The Complete Proficiency Practice Tests

2

Peter May

Heinemann English Language Teaching
A division of Heinemann Publishers (Oxford) Ltd
Halley Court, Jordan Hill, Oxford OX2 8EJ

OXFORD MADRID ATHENS PARIS
FLORENCE PRAGUE SÃO PAULO
CHICAGO MELBOURNE AUCKLAND
SINGAPORE TOKYO IBADAN GABORONE
JOHANNESBURG PORTSMOUTH (NH)

ISBN 0 435 28806 7 – without key
ISBN 0 435 28807 5 – with key

© Peter May 1992

First published 1992

Cassette produced by James Richardson at Studio AVP
Designed by Mike Brain

Illustrations: Laura Potter

Typeset by Wyvern Typesetting
Printed and bound in Great Britain by Thomson Litho Ltd., East Kilbride, Scotland

94 95 96 10 9 8 7 6 5 4 3

CONTENTS

THE CERTIFICATE OF PROFICIENCY   1
The Examination Papers   1
Getting more marks   2
Questions and answers about Paper 3 Use of English   2

ACKNOWLEDGEMENTS

The author would like to thank the students, teachers and librarians of the British Institute for Young Learners, Madrid; everyone at the Centre de Langues, Luxembourg; Jill Florent, Karen Jacobs, Sue Jones and Xanthe Sturt Taylor of Heinemann International. The Publishers would like to thank Jacky Newbrook, Tony Robinson, Judith Ash, Helen Pearce and the students of the Regent School of English, London; and Deborah Fenn and students of Anglo World, Oxford.

We would like to thank the following for permission to reproduce copyright material: c. Margaret Atwood 1991, extract 'Isis In Darkness' (p. 8); Jonathan Cape Publishers Ltd, 'London Fields', Martin Amis (p. 28); Sarah Charles, 'Gifts for the Get Up and Go Set' (p. 104); Daily Telegraph, 'Burn-out and the Superbabies', Ian Bell (November 1987) (p. 69); The Guardian, 'Tale of Soft-topped Driver', Tim Atkin (April 1990) (p. 13); Richard Boston, 'Now Where Was I' (December 1990) (p. 9); 'Black Becomes African American', W. J. Weatherby (p. 64); 'Perpetuating an Error', H. Whewell (January 1990) (p. 24); 'Uropi New Lingua Franca', P. Webster (January 1990) (p. 62), 'In Search of Greener Politics' (February 1990) (p. 46); Home Office, Crime Prevention Advertisement, 'If you think you're being followed what steps should you take?' (p. 21); The Independent, 'Innocents Who Can't Help Confessing', Jolyon Jenkins (January 1990) (p. 51); 'The True Value of Railways' (August 1990) (p. 49); 'How Travelling Becomes a Journey into Illness', Magdalen Russell (August 1990) (p. 98); 'A Pain in the Hand or Worker Hysteria', Mark Halliley (August 1989) (p. 103); Ruth Jacobs, 'Organic Gardening – A Beginner's Guide', (p. 79); Maev Kennedy, 'World's Biggest Iceberg' (p. 46); Cassandra Kent, '142 Door to Door Sales' (p. 104); Jenny Lecoat, 'Bad Mouthing' (p. 102); Hilary Lawson, 'Conspiracy in the Air' (p. 46); Nature Times News Service, c. Macmillan Magazines Ltd, 'Why Sleepwalkers May be Awake' (p. 44); The Observer, 'Hard Graff for a Piece of the Action', Cynthia Rose (April 1990) (p. 105); 'Haunted by the Grim Reaper of Winston-Salem', Andrew Stephen (February 1990) (p. 6); 'Solutions', Fred Pearce (April 1990) (p. 100); 'Policeman's Lot is not a Violent One', Michael Prestage (March 1990) (p. 30); 'Why Women Go to Work', Jean Carr (August 1989) (p. 103); Observer Magazine, 'Cold Feet', Simon Hoggart (April 1990) (p. 32); Peter Palmer, 'They Die, You Die' (WWF advertisement/Ogilvy & Mather) (p. 79); Penguin Books Ltd; 'Death of a Havard Man' taken from 'Dead Certainties', Simon Schama (p. 42); Robert Sandall, 'Taking the Hiss Out of the Sound of the Fifties' (p. 26); The Spectator, 3 extracts by John Casey (March 1989) p. 59); The Sun, '10 Great Ways to Get Your Own Back!', Ingrid Millar (September 1990) (p. 106); The Sunday Times, 'The Greenhouse Effect: Cold Logic or a Lot of Hot Air?', Richard North (August 1990) (p. 46); The Times, 'Fourth Leader' (September 1987) (p. 72).

While every effort has been made to trace the owners of copyright material in this book, there have been cases where the publishers have been unable to locate the sources. We would be grateful to hear from anyone who recognises their material and who is unacknowledged.

Photographs: Collections/Brian Shuel (p. 19, t), Impact Photos (Dod Miller–p. 38, b); Alain Le Garsmeur–p. 58, b), S & O Matthews (p. 78, bl), Network Photographers/Mike Goldwater (p. 78, t) Popperfoto (p. 58, tl), Science Photo Library (p. 78, br), Frank Spooner Pictures (p. 19, bl; p. 19, br), Zefa (p. 38, tr; P. 38, tl; p. 58, tr).
Key: l=left, c=centre, r=right, t=top, b=bottom

Illustrations: Laura Potter

THE CERTIFICATE OF PROFICIENCY

THE EXAMINATION PAPERS

Proficiency consists of five papers:

Paper 1: Reading Comprehension (1 hour)
40 multiple choice questions: you choose one of four possible answers to each one.
Section A consists of 25 questions that test your knowledge of vocabulary – including antonyms and synonyms; collocations; modal and phrasal verbs – and grammatical rules.

Section B has 15 questions on three or more texts, which may be taken from a variety of sources including novels, reports, advertising, brochures, newspapers, magazines and information leaflets. They test your understanding of the general meaning, as well as detail. Some questions test your ability to appreciate style and register, infer, and recognise the writer's intention.

Paper 2: Composition (2 hours)
You choose from five topics to write two compositions of up to 350 words each. The first three are descriptive, discursive and narrative titles, the fourth is based on a specific task and may be a little shorter, while the fifth is based on the optional set books.

Accuracy, fluency, appropriacy and range of expression, organisation and relevance to the topic are among the aspects of your writing which are tested.

Paper 3: Use of English (2 hours)
Section A includes a short text with one-word gaps to be filled in, as well as transformation and sentence completion exercises to test your active control of language.

Section B consists of a text followed by about fifteen open-ended questions. It tests your comprehension of the passage and ability to interpret it, in addition to your summarising skills.

Paper 4: Listening Comprehension (about 30 minutes)
There are usually four texts on cassette which are played twice. They include public announcements, conversations, broadcasts, discussions and telephone calls. The number of speakers varies, as do their accents.

While you listen, you fill in the answer sheet by, for example, labelling, blank-filling, matching information and answering multiple choice or true/false questions.

You are tested for your ability both to understand overall meaning and to extract specific detail, as well as to interpret attitudes and intentions from stress and intonation patterns.

Paper 5: Interview (about 15–20 minutes)
You can do the interview individually or in a group of two or three. If you are with other candidates you speak both to them and the examiner. A second examiner may be present as an assessor.

There are normally three parts, all linked by a common theme. First you are asked to discuss what you see in one or more photographs, and talk about related topics. Then you are shown a short passage and asked where it probably comes from, who is speaking to whom, or who it is written for, what its purpose is and so on. Finally, there is a discussion, roleplay or simulation, which may be based on a visual prompt such as a diagram or a written statement. You also have the option of talking about one of the set books.

You are tested throughout the interview for fluency, grammatical accuracy, pronunciation of sentences, pronunciation of individual sounds, interactive communication and vocabulary resource.

GETTING MORE MARKS

Proficiency is a test of your overall ability in English, so your grade is determined by the total number of marks you get in the five Papers, not the number of Papers you pass. You should still, however, aim for a good mark on every Paper: to pass you will need at least 40% on the Composition and about 60% on the other Papers. The maximum possible is 180 marks, divided up as shown below.

Reading Comprehension: There is one mark for each correct answer in Section A; two marks for each in Section B, so spend more time on questions 26–40 than on 1–25. In Section A imagine the situation in which the sentence would be used; in Section B think about where the text might be taken from. Always put an answer (one only, of course) even if you have to guess – all marks for Reading Comprehension are adjusted on the assumption that a certain percentage will be the result of good luck! The possible total of 55 marks for the Paper is scaled down to 40.

Composition: Each is marked out of 20. Do not concentrate on one composition at the expense of the other, as it is much easier to get enough marks on both compositions rather than try to get those extra few marks from one good composition. And if you write too much, the examiners might only mark the first 350 words or so; while if your composition is too short it may be marked out of 15, or even less. The total for the Paper is 40.

For more information, see *The Complete Proficiency Practice Tests 1*, page 5.

Use of English: Spend more time on Section A than on Section B as it carries more marks. In Section A, more than one answer may sometimes be possible, but you will not get any more marks for giving it. In questions 2, 4 and 5, though, marks may be given for **part** of the correct answer – so write in as much as you can of every one. Remember to leave plenty of time for the summary at the end of Section B as it often has 10 or more marks. The possible total of about 80 marks for the Paper is scaled down to 40.

Listening Comprehension: Use every spare second to form an impression of what you are going to hear: look at the questions and listen carefully to the introduction to each piece for clues to the situation and the speakers. Where there are options such as True/False or Yes/No (and for some simple one-word or single-figure answers) only half a mark is given – so do not spend so long on these as, for example, on multiple choice questions. And remember, as with Reading Comprehension, never to leave this type of answer blank – the guessing factor is taken into account where two or four options are given. The total for the Paper is adjusted to 20 marks.

Interview: To get good marks you will need to take an active part in discussions (which often include more abstract topics), use quite a wide range of structures and vocabulary, speak clearly and coherently, and not be unreasonably hesitant. That might sound a lot but in practice it just means communicating effectively with the examiner and (if you are in a group) other candidates – and don't worry about slips of the tongue or the odd mistake: native speakers make them too! Each of the six scales has a maximum of 5 marks: out of the 30 possible an adequate mark would be 18. The total for the Paper is adjusted to 40 marks.

For more information, see *The Complete Proficiency Practice Tests 1*, pp 5–6.

QUESTIONS AND ANSWERS ABOUT PAPER 3 USE OF ENGLISH

Here are the answers to some questions asked by candidates.

Is Use of English the most important part of the exam?
You can see above how many marks are given for each Paper. Use of English has the same number as Reading Comprehension, Composition and Interview. The examiners do point out, though, that the biggest difference between strong and weak candidates is often on this Paper; so check your Paper 3 percentage on the first Practice Test and make a special effort with Use of English if you are well below the target.

Is doing practice tests the only way to improve my Use of English?
As with any kind of test a certain amount of practice can greatly improve examination performance. You also need to read as much English as possible and work on your writing skills, as well as broadening your knowledge of – and ability to use – more complex grammatical structures. When you are practising Section A exercises, use your mistakes to identify your weaknesses and then check with a good grammar book.

Do we need a minimum mark in each part of the test?
No. You do not have to get a specific pass mark for the Paper as a whole, much less for every part, although you should aim at a reasonable number of marks for each rather than rely on doing particularly well in your 'favourite' part.

Which exercises in Section A have most marks, and which the least?
Question 1 – the gap-fill – has 20 marks: a large proportion of the total for the Paper. There may be two or even three marks for some of the 8 items in questions 2 and 4. There are usually only 6 items in question 3 and it is rare for more than one mark to be given for each. Bear these differences in mind when you decide how much time to spend on each question.

Do they deduct marks for wrong answers?
No. You have everything to gain and nothing to lose from putting an answer.

Can we fill in gaps in question 1 with half of a hyphenated word?
Only if the hyphen is given: although in practice the examiners avoid the possibility of this happening when they set the questions.

How can I tell which have more marks in transformation exercises?
Only by doing them! Always check you have made all the necessary changes to the sentence, including such 'secondary' ones as modifying time expressions for reported speech, leaving out the agent in passive sentences and turning one part of speech into another. Complex changes such as subject/auxiliary inversion after adverbials often carry two or more marks.

If you write two possible answers and one of them is correct while the other one isn't, do you get any marks?
No, you don't get any! Even if you give two completely correct answers only one of them will count, so don't waste time trying to think up more than one answer.

Do we have to follow the order of the sections?
You can do the sections, and each part of them, in any order you wish. The fact that more marks are given for Section A, though, may mean it does make sense to do it first. Some people prefer to do the summary in Section B before they write their answers to the individual questions: they like to form a general picture of the text before they go into detail and feel that this order helps them do so. But the final decision is yours.

Should we write the question at the beginning of the answer?
No. You don't get any marks for doing so and you might make mistakes if you try to rewrite questions like 'What is meant by . . .?' or 'What . . . is referred to by . . .?'. It also wastes valuable time. Just give the answer as concisely as you can.

Are the texts in Section B always from books?
No. As in Reading and Listening Comprehension, the texts are taken from a wide range of sources. Reading lots of different kinds of English will help prepare you for this.

Can we use words from the text in our answers?
Yes. You are not expected to try to rephrase everything from the passage: in many cases this would be impossible because true synonyms are rare in English. On the other hand, you will lose marks if you simply copy your answers from the text: remember that you are being tested on **your** use of English, not the text writer's! Use your common sense and put it in your own words where you think you are expected to.

Is all the answer to a question in one part of the text?
Sometimes not. You should always look elsewhere for more points or clues, particularly in questions that begin 'Why . . .', 'What . . ., 'How . . .' or 'In what ways . . .' etc.

Is it better to leave a gap or to write a word which you're not sure of?
When you write in your first language you don't leave gaps so don't do it in English! Use a phrase to explain what you mean, or if you're not sure of what you've written add something like – 'if that is the right word' –.

Can we add our own ideas to the summary?
No. The points must be taken only from the text and you should never add your own opinions about them. Paper 2 Composition and Paper 5 Interview are more the places for using your imagination and expressing your feelings!

Do we have to summarise all of the text?
Sometimes you do, other times you are asked to summarise only part of it. Read the instructions very carefully to make sure you get it right!

What happens if I run out of time on Section B?
Write in note form. Especially in the summary, some marks are given for the number of points from the text which you include. But by the time you take the exam you should have used the tests in this book to get your timing right!

Are some examiners stricter than others?
As in the case of compositions, every examiner's marking is carefully monitored and every candidate's marks is compared with those he or she obtained on other Papers in order to make the examination as fair as possible for all candidates.

For more information see *The Complete Proficiency Practice Tests 1*, page 3.

TEST ONE

PAPER 1 READING COMPREHENSION 1 hour

SECTION A

In this section you must choose the word or phrase which best completes each sentence. **On your answer sheet** *indicate the letter* **A, B, C** *or* **D** *against the number of each item 1 to 25 for the word or phrase you choose.*

1 News of the conflict _____ *D* _____ a dramatic fall on the stock exchange.

   A led   **B** based   **C** incited   **D** prompted

2 It's the third day in a _____ *B* _____ that the match has had to be put off.

   A line   **B** row   **C** file   **D** succession

3 The _____ *A* _____ formed band will first play two dates in Rotterdam.

   A newly   **B** lately   **C** ultimately   **D** latterly

4 The President's press _____ *A* _____ is now so large it needs its own plane.

   A body   **B** corps   **C** gang   **D** media

5 Somebody _____ *D* _____ the same issue at our last meeting.

   A lifted   **B** roused   **C** elevated   **D** raised

6 The complexity of some fraud cases was used as a _____ *B* _____ to abolish the right to trial by jury.

   A motive   **B** pretext   **C** loophole   **D** warrant

7 The findings of the report marked the _____ *C* _____ of the end for the industry.

   A starting   **B** commencing   **C** beginning   **D** dawning

8 A spokeswoman expressed disappointment _____ *A* _____ the level of response to the appeal.

   A at   **B** on   **C** in   **D** to

9 He was no _____ *A* _____ to hardship, having grown up in a shanty town on the outskirts of the city.

   A stranger   **B** outsider   **C** unknown   **D** foreigner

10 Observers feel that the _____ *C* _____ of his tolerance has already been reached.

   A peak   **B** top   **C** limit   **D** extreme

11 So far there's no _____ *B* _____ on who carried out the attack.

   A account   **B** word   **C** advice   **D** sentence

12 The Minister has so far resisted _____ *A* _____ for the re-introduction of hanging.

   A calls   **B** requirements   **C** claims   **D** applications

13 A global market will only come about when trade _____ *D* _____ have fallen.

   A walls   **B** checks   **C** blockades   **D** barriers

14 They rightly complain that nearly all the newspapers are _____ C _____ against them.

    A biased   **B** unfair   **C** subjective   **D** partial

15 The days of the government have clearly been _____ A _____ ever since the scandal broke.

    A counted   **B** numbered   **C** figured   **D** enumerated

16 Before you enter _____ A _____ any agreement make sure you get legal advice.

    A into   **B** for   **C** upon   **D** in

17 We _____ C _____ need someone who can look after the financial side of things.

    A awfully   **B** well   **C** badly   **D** dearly

18 After getting up at seven every day of the week, we like to _____ B _____ on Sunday mornings.

    A sleep over   **B** lie in   **C** stay up   **D** dream around

19 The recent _____ D _____ in consumer spending has led to fears of even higher interest rates.

    A soar   **B** expansion   **C** ascent   **D** upsurge

20 By setting up a huge factory near Leningrad, they hope to break _____ B _____ the Russian market.

    A up   **B** into   **C** down   **D** out

21 To be quite honest, I'm not all _____ A _____ keen on going there.

    A so   **B** very   **C** that   **D** really

22 The riot was _____ D _____ off by the announcement of higher food prices.

    A fired   **B** rifled   **C** shot   **D** triggered

23 The first _____ A _____ on tonight's phone-in is on line six.

    A caller   **B** speaker   **C** ringer   **D** talker

24 They thought it was all over but they could not have been _____ D _____ wrong.

    A as   **B** less   **C** so   **D** more

25 There was yet another _____ C _____ of violence late last night.

    A outpouring   **B** outrage   **C** outbreak   **D** outlet

21 / 25

SECTION B

In this section you will find after each of the passages a number of questions or unfinished statements about the passage, each with four suggested answers or ways of finishing. You must choose the one which you think fits best according to the passage. **On your answer sheet** *indicate the letter* **A**, **B**, **C** *or* **D** *against the number of each item* **26** *to* **40** *for the answer you choose. Give* **one answer only** *to each question. Read each passage right through before choosing your answers.*

FIRST PASSAGE

Last month, John Dillard Reynolds threw himself off the eleventh floor of a hotel in Florida. He was a gentle, decent man. But like so many others in Winston-Salem – like the tobacco farmers themselves, for instance – he knew that he was a living paradox. He knew that his grandfather had unwittingly played a major part in the deaths of far more people than had been killed in all the wars this century; that he himself was living off the profits from something that caused more deaths every year than cocaine, heroin, alcohol, fires, car crashes, murders and suicides combined. Or so a 390-page, inch-thick report published here last week assured us.

Reynolds, like most who make profits from what is a killer industry, would probably have refused to believe such unpalatable truths. But in this country alone, the report said, 3.6 million years of life are lost each year because of smoking – at an annual medical cost of $52 billion.

Reynold's grandfather was haunted by an instinct that the modern cigarette he so successfully marketed was somehow harmful to its users, but feared the problem lay in the paper rather than the tobacco. His son and heir, a two-packets-a-day man, died wretchedly at 58 from emphysema – gasping for breath in an oxygen tank. And last month his grandson, John Dillard, continued the sadly allegorical familial tale that personifies part of the twentieth century's greatest tragedy – the tobacco addiction that has claimed the lives of so many.

The irony of it all is that while the President flies dramatically to Columbia for a drugs summit, exhorting poor farmers to stop producing 'immoral' coca plants, his own Administration is subsidising US tobacco farmers to the tune of well over $100m a year. The moral message from America to the world is that the farmers of Bolivia, Colombia and Peru should grow more 'useful' crops. To that end the Administration is giving $2.2bn in aid over five years to the triumvirate of countries to help them correct their sinful ways and stop corrupting America's youth – as America sees it.

Yet, such is the perversity of life and the overriding force of commercial interests, that is precisely what the respectable domestic tobacco industry is trying to do here itself. It spends more than that per year in advertising, flogging respectability and targeting those social groups least resistant to its blandishments – which means children, teenagers, the poor, ethnic minorities, and women.

And as even they become better educated, so the tobacco companies turn their attention abroad. The race is now on to capture the hearts and lungs of the Third World and financial powerhouses of the Far East.

26 The report _~D~_   2

    A says that smoking kills between three
        and four million people a year.

    B claims that smoking has caused almost
        as many deaths as World War Two.

    C angered John Dillard Reynolds.

    D mentions the financial consequences of
        smoking.

27 How many members of the Reynolds family   c   ✗
have died from smoking?

    A None.

    B One.

    C Two.

    D Three.

28 Reynold's grandfather   ~D~   ✗

    A knew how many deaths he was
        responsible for.

    B did not care how many people died.

    C did not know why people died from
        smoking.

    D tried to make cigarettes safer.

29 The most money is being spent on   D   2

    A subsidies for US tobacco farmers.

    B subsidies for Latin American tobacco
        farmers.

    C US assistance for Bolivia, Colombia and
        Peru.

    D marketing by US cigarette companies.   ~D~

30 The writer accuses American tobacco   A   2
companies of

    A behaving no better than drug dealers.   ~B~

    B only being interested in rich customers.

    C ruining Latin American farmers.

    D encouraging the production of drugs in
        South America.

6/10

SECOND PASSAGE

All this was taking place, not in the ancient Middle Kingdom of the Egyptians, but in flat, dingy Toronto, on Spadina Avenue, at night, among the darkened garment factories and delicatessens and bars and pawnshops. It was a lament, and a celebration. Richard had never heard anything like it.

He sat back in his chair, fingering his patchy beard, trying as hard as he could to find this girl and her poetry trivial, overdone and pretentious. But he couldn't manage it. She was brilliant, and he was frightened. He felt his own careful talent shrivelling to the size of a dried bean.

The expresso machine did not go on once. After she'd finished there was a silence, before the applause. The silence was because people didn't know what to make of it, how to take it, this thing, whatever it was, that had been done to them. For a moment she had transformed reality, and it took them a breath to get it back.

Richard stood up, pushing past the bared legs of the woman poet. He didn't care any more who she might know. He went over to where Salena had just sat down, with a cup of coffee brought to her by Max.

'I liked your poems,' he managed to get out.

'Liked? Liked?' He thought she was making fun of him, although she wasn't smiling. '*Liked* is so margarine. How about *adored*?'

'Adored, then,' he said, feeling like an idiot twice over – for having said *liked* in the first place, and for jumping through her hoop in the second. But he got his reward. She asked him to sit down.

Up close her eyes were turquoise, the irises dark-ringed like a cat's. In her ears were blue-green ear-rings in the shape of scarabs. Her face was heart-shaped, her skin pale; to Richard, who had been dabbling in the French Symbolists, it evoked the word *lilac*. The shawl, the darkly outlined eyes, the ear-rings – few would have been able to pull it off. But she acted as if this was just her ordinary get up. What you'd wear any day on a journey down the Nile, 5,000 years ago.

It was of a piece with her performance – bizarre, but assured. Fully achieved. The worst of it was that she was only eighteen.

'That's a lovely shawl.' Richard attempted. His tongue felt like a beef sandwich.

'It's not a shawl, it's a table-cloth,' she said. She looked down at it, stroked it. Then she laughed a little. 'It's a shawl *now*.'

Richard wondered if he should dare to ask – what? If he could walk her home? Did she have anything so mundane as a home? But what if she said no? While he was deliberating, Max the bullet-headed coffee hack walked over and put a possessive hand on her shoulder, and she smiled up at him. Richard didn't wait to see if it meant anything. He excused himself, and left.

He went back to his rented room and composed a sestina to her. It was a dismal effort; it captured nothing about her. He did what he had never before done to one of his poems. He burnt it.

31 The poetry reading was held in

   A a cafe.
   B France.
   C North Africa.
   D Salena's house.

32 What effect did Salena's poems have?

   A The audience hated them.
   B Richard felt they were better than his poems.
   C Richard felt his were better.
   D The audience was bored.

33 How does Salena react when Richard speaks to her?

   A She imposes her will on his.
   B She starts to get changed.
   C She looks for someone else to talk to.
   D She tries to put him at his ease.

34 It is clear from the passage that Max and Salena

   A know each other.
   B dislike one another.
   C are in love with each other.
   D have never met before.

35 Salena makes Richard feel

   A confident.
   B indifferent.
   C superior.
   D inadequate.

THIRD PASSAGE

To save time at Newhaven the passport inspection was carried out on the ship. It was four o'clock in the morning by the time my turn in the queue was approaching. Not far ahead of me was an Asian, aged about 60. He was smartly dressed and had masses of documents. Even so, he was being grilled. What was the address of the Mr Patel he was going to stay with? How much money did he have? How long was he staying? Was he married? Did he have children . . .?

Not only was this almost elderly Asian being subjected to all sorts of questions the answers to which were clearly documented but it was late at night and he had been travelling for a long time. He was standing, while the young immigration officer was sitting. The judge sits, the defendant stands. The passport-holder is in the dock, and guilty until proved innocent.

Finally he was allowed through and it was the turn of two young Australians. Their passports were perused as if in search of pornography or narcotics. What was the purpose of their visit? Were they married? Where had they come from? Where were they going to stay? How long? How much money had they with them?

Now it was my turn. I had prepared to the best of my ability. For some reason I hadn't lost my tie, so I had put it on. As I approached I had my press card and my British Library ticket and my address book in hand. I offered them hesitantly while saying with as much confidence as I could muster, 'To come straight to the point, I've lost my passport.'

With scarcely a glance at my pitiful documents of identification he said, in a rather comforting tone, 'That's all right sir,' and I was through.

Sir, SIR. It will come as no surprise to anyone to be told that there are advantages in being middle-class, middle-aged, white and with an expensively acquired Standard English accent. If you're not white, and you're aged less than 25, and you haven't got a tie, and you drop your aitches, and you've got long hair and you want to be called Sir, then you're going about things the wrong way, buddy.

---

36 According to the author, the older man was treated like that because he   C

  A spoke with an accent.
  B was poor.
  C was an Asian.
  D did not have a passport.

37 People wishing to enter the country were questioned   c

  A in court.
  B at sea.
  C in the harbour.
  D at Newhaven.

38 When he spoke to the immigration officer, the author felt   A

  A nervous.
  B superior.
  C sad.
  D impatient.

39 One reason why he was treated with more respect than the others was that he   A

  A was travelling from a different country.
  B had been to a certain type of school.
  C was extremely rich.
  D was married and had children.

40 The author of this passage is   B

  A an immigrant.
  B a journalist.
  C a tourist.
  D a judge.

6/10

43/55

PAPER 2 COMPOSITION 2 hours

*Write **two only** of the following composition exercises. Your answers must follow exactly the instructions given. Write in pen, not pencil. You are allowed to make alterations, but make sure your work is clear and easy to read.*

1 Describe a scheme in your country designed to protect or improve the environment. (About 350 words)

2 'A university education should be available to anyone who wants it.' How far do you agree with this statement? (About 350 words)

3 Tell the story of something that happened to you which you feel was unfair. (About 350 words)

4 Your home has been burgled. Write a formal statement for the police using the points on this checklist as prompts. (About 300 words)

GREATER MANCHESTER CONSTABULARY
Larceny

- address & type of property;
- estimated time of theft;
- occupants of building;
- method of entry;
- items stolen;
- damage done;
- insurance details.

5 Set books.

PAPER 3 USE OF ENGLISH 2 hours

SECTION A

1 *Fill each of the numbered blanks in the passage with **one** suitable word.*

The routine for dispensing medicines has long resembled a game of Chinese whispers. The doctor
scribbles a prescription (1), the pharmacist makes a stab at interpreting this, then counts
out (2) some pills by hand into a brown bottle. The bottle is given a tiny label (3)
which begins to smudge and fade almost immediately, and will peel off (4) after a week
in the bathroom cabinet. By the time you're halfway through (5) the course of tablets
neither (6) the doctor, the pharmacist nor the patient has any idea what medicine is being
taken (7).

Help is at hand (8) from the EC which is insisting that all drugs must (9) be
dispensed like contraceptive pills packet (10), in their own printed packs. Each pack will
contain the number of tablets required for an average course and will by (11) law
contain an information sheet about the product, its effects and side effects.

Some (12) kind of patient information has taken a long time developing (13). Most
resistance stems at (14) the belief that listing the side effects will encourage people to
develop those problems and put (15) them off taking the tablets. Happily, most people
are actively reassured with (16) a list of possible side effects they haven't developed. The
evidence is that patients are more likely (17) to carry on (18) taking a product if
they have clear information about it. Furthermore (19), a recent study in America showed that
patients are more likely to take an inferior medicine accompanied by information than a
demonstrably superior product with no (20) information sheet.

14/20

2 *Finish each of the following sentences in such a way that it is as similar as possible in meaning to the sentence printed before it.*

Example: Nobody had given it any thought before then.
Answer: It was only *then that anybody gave it any thought.*

a Who was the previous owner of the vehicle?

Who did the vehicle belong to before?

b You'll be in serious trouble if you do that again.

Do that again and you'll be in serious trouble.

c The business will never make money, even if you invest a fortune in it.

1 However _____ much you invest in the business, it will never make money.

d A fence was put up so that livestock would not stray onto the road.

1 To prevent _livestock straying onto the road, a fence was put up._

e They would have failed if they hadn't taken the extra supplies.

3 Not to _have taken the extra supplies would have led to their failure._

f The victims' names were withheld until relatives had been informed.

2 Only after _relatives had been informed were the victim's names released._

g 'What were you up to last night?' he asked her.

2 He asked her what _she had been up to the previous night._

h The Chairman has requested that I should speak to you on his behalf.

1 The Chairman wishes _me to speak to you on his behalf._

12/12

3 *Fill each of the blanks with a suitable word or phrase.*

Example: I took it _for granted_ that you had been told already.

1 **a** We needn't go into details. Suffice _it to say_ that an accident has taken place.

1 **b** They seized several hostages and are reported _to have_ headed south.

× **c** He threatened _to phone / go_ to the police unless they turned the music down.

× **d** I was shocked by what we saw but she looked as if she _cared for / couldn't care_ less.

× **e** Were there _to have / be_ any further incidents, stronger measures would have to be considered.

½ **f** What a childish way to carry on! Why can't you _behave / act your_ age? (like someone of your)

2½/6

4 *For each of the sentences below, write a new sentence as similar as possible in meaning to the original sentence, but using the word given. This word **must not be altered** in any way.*

Example: Was it really necessary for you to shout like that?
have
Answer: *Did you really have to shout like that?*

a He believed he was helping people when he did that.
belief

½ His belief was that he was helping people when he did that.

b He just failed to break the world record.
succeed

2 He didn't quite succeed in breaking the world record.

c There is still an awful lot to do.
remains

½ An awful lot (still) remains to be done

d In just over a week it will be polling day.
    go

7 ½/12

✗   *In just over a week people will go voting.*

e She's too experienced a player to fall into that trap.
    enough

2   *As a player, she's experienced enough not to fall into that trap.*

f They will be charged with fraud and tax evasion.
    face

½   *They will (have to) face the charges of fraud and tax evasion.*

g He worked in the Treasury before he was appointed Chancellor.
    prior

1   *Prior to (being appointed) his appointment as Chancellor, he worked in the Treasury.*

h There's nobody else here so let's go home.
    seeing

1   *Let's go home seeing there's nobody else here.*

SECTION B

5 *Read the following passage, then answer the questions which follow it.*

Seduced by the prospect of carefree, soft-topped motoring, I bought an MGB Roadster last year. A piece of our heritage for only three thousand quid. I pictured myself swishing through the countryside in flat-cap and Aran sweater, joking with my girlfriends as our scarves played merrily in the wind.

Eagerly I joined a local MG owners' club. This is affiliated to the national MGOC, with its   5
network of 50,000 members. The monthly club newsletter carries captioned photographs of some of them, standing proudly by their Midgets: 'Swedish member Conny Sjoquist and girlfriend Caroline would like to thank Michael and Carol Bacon for their wonderful hospitality during their stay in England'. It even has it own Lonely Hearts column. Anyone fancy a 'Professionally cheesed-off commuter' seeking 'female to plan escapes from the rat-race'?   10

Fellow MG owners are preternaturally friendly. They exchange waves, flash their lights and swap dealers' telephone numbers. I was happy to be among them. I shelled out on a lapel badge, subscribed to a vintage car magazine and bought a pair of MG boxer shorts. No one could have been more enthusiastic.

On the club's first outing ('. . . the merry band of adventurers ventured farther and finally halted   15
at the Fox and Hounds, where all were fed and watered'), my car broke down. The week after, the battery was flat. This is helpfully situated under the passenger shelf. Removing it involves a balancing act with a piece of wire, while battery acid pours all over your feet. You get better at this. A month later one side of the car had to be rebuilt. The engine was next, seizing after a few hundred miles of summer motoring. Repairs had already cost more than the bloody car. When the   20
autumn rains started, my MG wouldn't. Friends got fed up pushing the thing. The interior always smelled of mould. There was so much water in the bottom at one point that I had a bath plug installed. My girlfriend had finally seen enough. She ran off with a Ford Fiesta owner from Cornwall.

One day I came to my senses. MGs are not meant to be driven. They are fetishes, not cars.   25
Motors for train spotters, obsessed with the minutiae of trim. The sort of people who spend years restoring a vintage rust-bucket, polishing the suspension with a toothbrush. Their cars even have names, for God's sake.

If you're feeling tempted by the sunshine and a bit of wanderlust, don't be. MGs are dismally slow, cramped, irritating, expensive to run and make a Trabant look environmentally sound. Still   30
hankering? Then perhaps you'd like to buy mine. I am prepared to accept considerably less than I paid for it.

a Why did the writer buy an MG?

fun iv convertible x cheap

He was "seduced" by the idea of driving a vintage car of which the roof could come down, and driving it in the countryside being dressed fashionably with his girlfriend by his side and their scarves flapping in the wind.

b What do the 'captioned photographs' (line 6) consist of?

\

The members and girlfriends 'standing by' their cars.

c What is a 'Lonely Hearts column'?

\

A page where bachelor or spinster members can write an advertisement to try and find an interested partner.

d What is meant by a 'Professionally cheesed-off commuter' (line 10)?

2

A person that travels to go to work, usually in an office, and who is unhappy to do so.

e In what ways did the writer show how 'enthusiastic' (line 14) he was?

3

He wore an MG badge on his lapel, "subscribed to a vintage car magazine and bought a pair of MG boxer shorts". He was also happy to copy the MG drivers' habits.

f What did they do at the 'Fox and Hounds'?

2

It was the writer first outing and his car broke down there. The members ate and drank water.

g Why does the writer use the word 'helpfully' on line 17 and what is implied by the sentence 'You get better at this.' (line 18)?

2

He uses it for pure sarcasm because the battery isn't at all in an easy place to reach. It is easier to pour battery acid on your feet than removing it by a careful balance helped with using a piece of wire.

h What did the writer have to do to the engine during the summer? Which word expresses his feelings about this?

2

The engine seized and had to be rebuilt. The writer felt depressed that "the repairs had <u>already cost more than</u> the <u>bloody car.</u>"

i What does 'wouldn't' mean on line 21?

1

The car refused to start when "the autumn rains" did.

j How was the plug (line 22) supposed to work? What did its installation lead to?

2

It was supposed to let ^{out}the water ^{retained} at the bottom⁵ of the car but its installation led to the writer's girlfriend to leave him, having had enough of that car, for someone else owning a modern car.

k What, according to the writer, should be done with MGs?

2

MGs should be in museums, only enthusiastics keep those old cars to renovate them and polish them carefully as a passionate hobby. However the cars shouldn't be driven.

l Why does the writer use the expression 'for God's sake' on line 28?

1

Giving a name to a car one can't drive without it breaking down seems foolish and enervating to the writer.

m What is the purpose of the reference to a 'Trabant' on line 30?

X

A Trabant is an old unreliable car built in the East knowing that it makes the vintage MGs look even worse; it is irony.

n Explain the meaning of 'Still hankering?' (line 30)

1

Knowing everything the writer said about the MGs does the reader keep an interest in those cars?

o In a paragraph of 70–90 words, describe the difficulties the writer had with his MG.

6½/7

+ (2)

The first difficulty occured on his first outing when the car <s>break</s> ^{BROKE} down, after that the battery went flat which caused him trouble to remove because it isn't placed to be easily accessible. Then one side of the body had to be rebuilt and so had the engine after a while. With the wet weather the car couldn't start and water accumulated in the car which made it smell bad. All those incidents caused his girlfriend to leave him and friends to be annoyed with him and his dodgy car.

PAPER 4   LISTENING COMPREHENSION   about 30 minutes

FIRST PART

*For questions **1–4** tick one of the boxes **A**, **B**, **C**, or **D**.*

1   People are most likely to be affected by noise from

    A   machines used in industry.

    B   strong winds or draughts.

    C   electronic equipment.

    D   other people's conversations.

A	
B	
C	
D	

2   Day says that noise

    A   sometimes helps people to work better.

    B   might not be as harmful to our ears as some people claim.

    C   may make relatively simple tasks more difficult.

    D   can make it impossible to use office telephones.

A	
B	
C	
D	

3   Studies in the United States seem to show that

    A   noise is only a problem if it is continuous.

    B   aircraft noise is less harmful than other kinds of noise.

    C   the effects of noise can be both mental and physical.

    D   noise is a cause of juvenile delinquency.

A	
B	
C	
D	

4   Day believes that research should now be done in

    A   schools.

    B   laboratories.

    C   people's homes.

    D   offices and factories.

A	
B	
C	
D	

SECOND PART

*For question **5**, fill in the missing information in the spaces provided by giving **brief** answers. One has already been filled in as an example.*

5   Proportion of sufferers in population about _____*1 in 12*_____

Obsessive washing syndrome named after **a** _____

Impossible to take shoplifter's **b** _____

Man feared he could not paint if he **c** _____

Man who climbed steps twice daily suffered from **d** _____

Newest phobia: being frightened of **e** _____

Likely no. of British agoraphobia sufferers: **f** _____

Approx. no. of male agoraphobics in UK: **g** _____

Some motorists unable to take **h** _____

Sufferer risked serious injury to get away from **i** _____

Suicidal woman drew **j** _____

THIRD PART

For questions 6–11 tick one of the boxes A, B, C, or D.

6 Which are immune to motion sickness?

    A   Children who can look at animals from the car.

    B   Men who have spent years at sea.

    C   People who travel in luxurious cars.

    D   None of the above.

A	
B	
C	
D	

7 Nausea

    A   occurs in isolation from other symptoms.

    B   forms part of a vicious circle.

    C   is due to unknown causes.

    D   cannot be treated.

A	
B	
C	
D	

8 Williams uses

    A   medicine, homeopathy, ginger and acupuncture.

    B   medicine, homeopathy and acupuncture.

    C   homeopathy and acupuncture.

    D   homeopathy, ginger and acupuncture.

A	
B	
C	
D	

9 According to the speaker, Sea Bands

    A   are a miracle cure.

    B   might be effective.

    C   are completely useless.

    D   could be dangerous.

A	
B	
C	
D	

10 Military sufferers of motion sickness

    A   are very rare.

    B   cannot become pilots.

    C   usually overcome the problem.

    D   should never fly in helicopters.

A	
B	
C	
D	

11 When in cars, adult sufferers should

    A   never drive.

    B   always sit in the front.

    C   never close the windows.

    D   eat nothing.

A	
B	
C	
D	

FOURTH PART

12 *For question 12 tick whether you think the statements are **true** or **false**.*

		True	False
a	The panel is a U.S. Government organisation.		
b	Their decisions can affect the language.		
c	They include 'experts' in both written and spoken English.		
d	They are all purists.		
e	They can influence British English.		
f	One third reject the modern meaning of *decimate*.		
g	In 1969, the majority approved of *anxious* to mean *eager*.		
h	50% believe that *transpire* should lose its old meaning.		
i	The panel disapprove of mixing singular and plural forms.		
j	Most of them still reject the split infinitive.		

PAPER 5 INTERVIEW

The theme of this Test is **Crime**.

1   **a**   Look at *one* of the photographs and describe:
- ☐ the setting
- ☐ the people
- ☐ what they seem to be doing

If you are doing the interview in a group, contrast the people and the offence with those in the others'.

    b   Now discuss:
- ☐ the reasons why some people become criminals
- ☐ how this can be prevented
- ☐ the relative seriousness of different types of crime

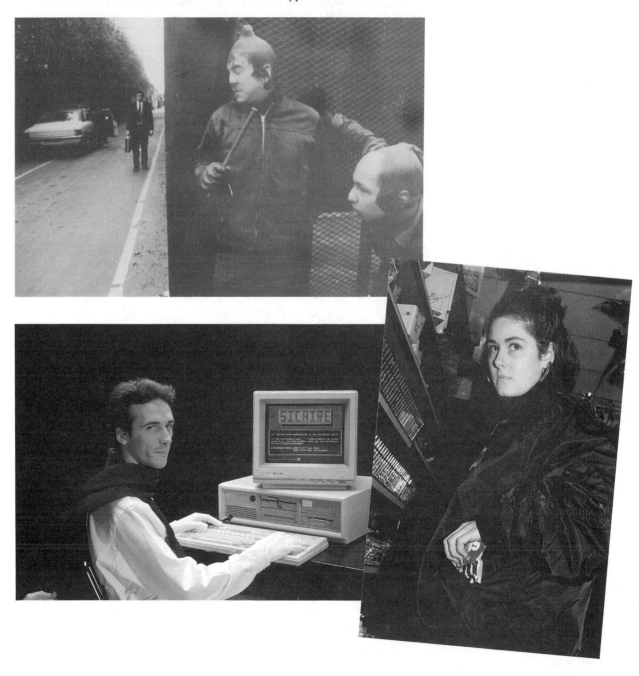

2   Study *one* of these passages. You may quote from it if you wish.

a   Although cheque card fraud still accounts for over half the £3 billion that crime costs UK companies every year while more than £200 million goes in bribes and an estimated £830 million is stolen by employees, it is product extortion – computer viruses and attempted blackmail – that is really taking off. Last year's figure topped £400 million, as reported cases more than doubled.

b   The thing is that people really are so stupid I mean they just leave motors lying around the place and then they get surprised when they go missing and they wonder how we did it when really it's dead easy, at any rate with most of them. But what you're really after is something smart, something that really motors – you know what I mean – so you can wind it up and leave them all for dead if they get after you.

c   In a country where people are encouraged to inform anonymously on anyone they have a grudge against and can accuse of tax dodging or welfare fiddling, where free phone calls are offered to shop those you dislike and think could be drink drivers, and where travel agents are requested to report customers they suspect might be 'involved in drugs', I was delighted to hear that a chain store's phone line for employees to denounce 'dishonest' colleagues has been dropped: during its 12-month trial period not a single call was received.

Where do you think the text is taken from?
Who do you think the speaker or writer might be?
What is the purpose of the text?
Discuss the content.

3 Do *one* of these tasks.

a Imagine the government has proposed that a curfew be imposed on young people in order (they say) to cut crime: everyone under 20 must be at home by 8pm every evening. Say what your feelings are. You can be for or against the proposal.

b Look at the text below and then discuss the following:

IF YOU THINK YOU'RE BEING FOLLOWED, WHAT STEPS SHOULD YOU TAKE?

About 94% of crimes are against property rather than people. But, not surprisingly, it is the remaining 6% that causes the most comment and concern. Although young men are more likely to be victims, it is women and the elderly who often feel at greater risk. Whoever you are, you'll feel more confident if you take the following advice:

1. CROSS THE STREET

If someone walking behind you is making you nervous, cross the street – more than once if necessary – to check your suspicions. If you are still worried, go quickly to a place with other people and call the police.

2. COVER-UP

Cover up expensive looking jewellery and keep your handbag close to your body. If someone does grab your bag, let it go rather than risk injury by fighting. (It's sensible to keep your house keys separately.)

3. AVOID SHORT-CUTS

Avoid short-cuts through dimly lit alleys or across waste ground.

4. FACE THE TRAFFIC

Walk facing the traffic so a car cannot pull up behind you unnoticed. You should also stay on the outside edge of the pavement, keeping away from bushes and dark buildings.

5. SHOUT IF THREATENED

If a car does approach you and you feel threatened, run in the opposite direction, making it more difficult for the driver to follow. (Don't be afraid to shout.)

6. EVEN CARRY A SCREECH ALARM

If you regularly walk home after dark, consider buying a screech alarm. Carry it in your hand, not in a bag where it would be difficult to reach in an emergency.

7. ARRANGE SAFE TRANSPORT

Try to arrange a lift home or book a taxi if you're going to be out late. Never hitch-hike or accept lifts from strangers.

8. VARY YOUR ROUTE

If you regularly go jogging or cycling, try to vary your route and time so you're less likely to be waylaid by an attacker.

9. SELF-DEFENCE CLASSES

Self-defence classes can increase your confidence. Ask your local police or employer if they run classes.

10. OVER A HUNDRED MORE IDEAS

You'll find a hundred more steps you can take to protect yourself, your family and your property in "Practical Ways to Crack Crime." For your free 44-page colour copy, send this coupon to: Home Office, PO Box 7000, Cirencester GL7 1RX or call

01-569 7000

Name _____
Address _____
_____
Postcode _____

CRIME
TOGETHER WE'LL CRACK IT

PRACTICAL WAYS TO CRACK CRIME HANDBOOK

☐ The reasons for some of the advice, e.g. keeping house keys separate, avoiding bushes and dark buildings.
☐ Which of the points would be useful, or useless, in your country; and why.
☐ Any further advice you would give.

TEST TWO

PAPER 1   READING COMPREHENSION   1 hour

SECTION A

In this section you must choose the word or phrase which best completes each sentence. **On your answer sheet** *indicate the letter* **A**, **B**, **C** *or* **D** *against the number of each item 1 to 25 for the word or phrase you choose.*

1 The manager lost _____ B _____ when his decision was overruled by his boss.

  A nerve   **B** face   **C** temper   **D** head

2 This government will never _____ A _____ to demands made by terrorists.

  A give in   **B** give over   **C** give out   **D** give up

3 It's about time they put a _____ A _____ to that kind of cheating.

  A stop   **B** curb   **C** termination   **D** finish

4 He lives alone and is so intent _____ D _____ his work that he sometimes forgets to eat.

  A of   **B** for   **C** on   **D** to

5 They carried on with their programme _____ A _____ attacks from vested interests.

  A in the face of   **B** for all that   **C** despite the fact that   **D** yet even so

6 Regular viewers won't need _____ D _____ of what comes next.

  A to remind   **B** remembering   **C** reminding   **D** to be remembered

7 The two leaders made a _____ D _____ declaration on the need for urgent measures.

  A tied   **B** mutual   **C** together   **D** joint

8 Personally I haven't seen them, but _____ D _____ they're something special.

  A according to   **B** even though   **C** out of the question   **D** by all accounts

9 The model that's just come out is a definite improvement _____ A _____ the old one.

  A on   **B** by   **C** in   **D** at

10 He claimed in court that he was not _____ D _____ for the injuries sustained by the plaintiff.

  A the cause   **B** guilty   **C** the culprit   **D** responsible

11 In the _____ C _____ majority of cases, no further action is taken.

  A broad   **B** huge   **C** vast   **D** wide

12 Stability in the region could be _____ D _____ affected by military aid to either side.

  A adversely   **B** hardly   **C** ill   **D** harmfully

13 Following the attempted coup, the situation _____ A _____ tense in the capital.

  A remains   **B** endures   **C** stays   **D** keeps

14 We must take _____ D _____ to ensure that nothing like this ever happens again.

  A paces   **B** strides   **C** trots   **D** steps

✓ **15** The most exciting ⎯⎯⎯C⎯⎯⎯ so far is a beautifully-preserved sixteenth-century ship's figurehead.

    A encounter   **B** meet   **C** find   **D** apprehension

✓ **16** News of the disaster brought the celebrations to ⎯⎯⎯B⎯⎯⎯ end.

    A the   **B** an   **C** some   **D** their

✓ **17** Even when the January sales are on, that place seems a bit ⎯⎯⎯D⎯⎯⎯ to me.

    A costly   **B** steep   **C** high   **D** pricey

✓ **18** Those who do not speak the official language have become a ⎯⎯⎯C⎯⎯⎯ minority.

    A prosecuted   **B** pestered   **C** persecuted   **D** pursued

✓ **19** Everyone in the earthquake zone is wondering how many more tremors there ⎯⎯⎯A⎯⎯⎯ .

    A are to come   **B** will be coming   **C** are coming   **D** are to have come

✗ **20** Since government aid began to be channelled in, new industries have started to ⎯⎯⎯C⎯⎯⎯ up all over the region.

    A leap   **B** jump   **C** rise   (**D** spring)

✓ **21** There's such a lot ⎯⎯⎯A⎯⎯⎯ that we've got to get it right this time.

    A at stake   **B** depending on   **C** in play   **D** by chance

✓ **22** Many ⎯⎯⎯B⎯⎯⎯ life has been lost through a moment's carelessness.

    A the   **B** a   **C** such   **D** this

✗ **23** Despite election promises of radical change, they ⎯⎯⎯D⎯⎯⎯ their reform programme as soon as they took office.

    A melted down   **B** smoothed down   (**C** watered down)   **D** turned down

✗ **24** We've asked ⎯⎯⎯A⎯⎯⎯ again to be allowed to visit the prisoners.

    A on and on   **B** ever and ever   **C** more and more   (**D** time and time)

✗ **25** It is not ⎯⎯⎯B⎯⎯⎯ to take equipment away from the premises.

    (**A** permitted)   **B** allowed   **C** let   **D** admitted

18/25

SECTION B

In this section you will find after each of the passages a number of questions or unfinished statements about the passage, each with four suggested answers or ways of finishing. You must choose the one which you think fits best according to the passage. **On your answer sheet**, *indicate the letter* **A**, **B**, **C** *or* **D** *against the number of each item* **26** *to* **40** *for the answer you choose. Give* **one answer only** *to each question. Read each passage right through before choosing your answers.*

FIRST PASSAGE

Whenever people in the advertising business fall to discussing the giants of their trade sooner or later they always get round to telling the tale of the man who saved the salmon cannery in South Alaska. It's a good tale and like all good tales well able to stand almost any amount of embellishment and embroidery. But I will leave all that to the readers' imagination and content myself here with the bare bones.

The cannery was modern, efficient, and with an exemplary management and a hard-working labour force. The river on which it stood was swift, clear and well-stocked with fish. There was just one snag. Due to some curious quirk of the local soil chemistry the flesh of the fish – though excellent in every other respect – was white rather than red. At a time when all its competitors were boosting their sales by emphasising the rich ruddiness of *their* products the Alaskan company found itself staring ruin in the face and as a last throw called in a well known New York ad man.

After barely a day on site the New York man announced that he had found the solution that promised salvation and the management assembled in the boardroom all agog to hear it. There was no need, said the ad man, for extensive refurbishments or reorganisations; no call either for expensive promotion campaigns. All that would be required was a small adjustment to the wording on the labels around the tins. If he could just be provided with one of the existing labels he would demonstrate what it was he had in mind. A label was at once produced and our ad man worked on it for only a minute or two before passing it back over the table. Clear across it in block letters he had written the simple message – THIS SALMON IS GUARANTEED *NOT* TO TURN RED IN THE TIN.

It's a good many years since I first heard that story and I don't suppose it was exactly new then so I had come to suppose that its hero was no longer with us. I was wrong. Just yesterday I came upon his handiwork on a tin of sardines bought at my local Co-op. The key normally provided with each tin was missing from this one and I was about to curse some careless packer when I noticed a diagonal overprint across the label. NEW TIN, it said, Simply Open with a Tin Opener.

Now I don't know if the Co-op has simply mislaid its entire stock of sardine tin-openers, which is not impossible, I suppose. Or perhaps some tight-lipped accountant has pointed out that thousands of pounds can be saved by leaving them off the sardine tins. What seems certain, however, is that our friend from across the water has been called in to put a gloss on things and that he followed his own tried and tested example. What can we expect to see from him next, I wonder. A car showroom with its latest economy model labelled NEW POWER UNIT. SIMPLY ATTACH HORSE?

26 The story of the salmon cannery

    A is the subject of bitter controversy.
    B is often spoilt by the person who tells it.
    C can be told in a variety of ways.
    D has been changed by the author of this text.

27 Before they saw the message on the label, the management were

    A resigned.
    B unhelpful.
    C excited.
    D confident.

28 The ad man's message implies that salmon

    A should always be white.
    B is only red when it is first caught.
    C changes colour when the tin is opened.
    D is naturally red in South Alaska.

29 The author of the passage thought that the ad man

    A was working for a different advertising agency.
    B had died.
    C now worked in the motor trade.
    D was employed by one of the Alaskan firm's competitors.

30 The ad man

    A failed to increase the cannery's sales.
    B angered consumer groups.
    C improved the quality of tinned salmon.
    D seems to have used a similar idea in Britain.

31 Overall, the author's attitude to the ad man is one of

    A harsh criticism.
    B complete hero-worship.
    C considerable admiration.
    D moderate scepticism.

SECOND PASSAGE

When it comes to 1950s vintage blues, soul and rock 'n' roll, all our modern preoccupations with clarity, smoothness and high fidelity slam straight into the sharp end of the question of authenticity. How should we listen today to music which was originally – and famously – recorded on primitive equipment in improvised studios and with what often sounds like a cavalier disregard for sound quality and accuracy of performance?

Pop records of the 1950s were designed specifically to be played on the radio and listened to in the home on small speakers. Dynamics which drew attention to high trebles, low basses or quiet bits diminished a song's impact (that is, loudness) and were dealt with accordingly at the mixing stage. Any vocal or guitar performance was liable to be coated with crude but ear-catching echo effects. Hiss, ambient noises, distortion and mistakes could all be safely buried in there somewhere – and teenagers around the world equipped with Dansette record players and tiny radios would either not notice or not care.

This leaves Roger Armstrong, owner of the Ace label – which specialises in re-releases, increasingly on CD – with an interpretative dilemma. 'What do you do? Try to re-create an actual performance, or just re-create what people are already used to hearing, which means the radio tapes? I believe our job is to say: this is what the performance was like. We're rewriting history to create something that, if you played it to the original producer, he'd say, God I wish I'd had the equipment to make it sound like that.'

By rummaging through the dusty vaults of major record companies, Armstrong and other fellow historians seek out 'raw' studio tapes, which can then be renovated, typically by tweaking up treble and bass frequencies to add greater definition and separation.

But such highlighting procedures can create problems as fast as they solve them. As Neil Slaven, a producer who cleans up old tapes for another specialist vintage label, Charly, points out, his Fifties forebears 'were actually recording events in a room, not just instruments and voices'. Armstrong regularly agonises over tape hiss. 'Remove hiss and you may be taking out the drummer splashing away on his ride cymbal. There's a constant trade-off between the muscial information you're losing and the sound quality you gain.' The perception of quality, of course, involves psycho-acoustic value-judgements and is, as such, an inexact science.

32 According to the text, the present-day   B   ʔ
listener has to decide whether

   A the current obsession with perfect sound
quality is worrying.
   B quality is more important than
maintaining the original sound.
   C compact disc recordings are more
authentic than those on vinyl.
   D it is worth listening to 1950s music at all.

33 The sound quality of 1950s recordings   D   ʔ

   A was improved in the studio by increasing
the volume.
   B was very poor except for the singers and
guitarists.
   C covered up all the imperfections.
   D reflected the audio equipment used by
listeners.

34 The Ace label   C   ʔ

   A is a chain of record shops.
   B concentrates on new bands and songs.
   C issues new copies of old records.
   D was a 1950s record company.

35 The problem Armstrong faces is that   A   ʔ

   A his recordings are different from the
original tapes.
   B The 1950s producers resent what he is
doing to their recordings.
   C people are bored with hearing the same
old songs.
   D he cannot change the original tapes.

36 New problems are created because   c   X

   A there can be no objective definition of
the ideal sound.
   B it is cheaper to leave out the sound of
certain instruments.
   C improved sound quality brings out
unwanted background noises.
   D some people believe that hiss should
always be eliminated.

8/10

THIRD PASSAGE

Guy linked up again with his courier or expeditor at the airport in New London. Here he was told that, if he wished, he could get an air-taxi straight to Newark. With luck he might catch an earlier Concorde and shave perhaps half a day off his journey. The courier smiled and twinkled potently; everything was possible; his was the maximum-morale specialism of deeply expensive travel. At this point he paid off the chauffeur, whose disaffection remained secure against Guy's reckless tip. Outside in the warm dusk the light was the colour of a grinning pumpkin, Halloween light, promising trick or treat.

Before he retired to the Celebrity Lounge (there would be a slight delay) Guy wandered the concourses, full of love's promiscuous interest, among pantsuit and stretchslack America. Even though there was said to be less of it now, the human variety on display, with its dramatic ratios of size and colouring, still impressed and affected him. It was true that you did see signs of uniformity (one nation), all the people wearing off-white smocks and pink, gymkhana-sized rosettes, like that family over there, four of them, in perfect-family formation, man and woman and boy and girl, each with the squeamish smile of the future . . . Guy threw away his painkillers – their tubes and sachets. Everywhere young women looked at him with kindness. But of course there was only one woman who could really kill his pain. The eyes of certain faces, children's faces, made him wonder whether this whole adventure of his, so agitated and inspired, and so climactic, wasn't just a way of evading the twentieth century or the planet or what the one had done to the other.

37 What was the chauffeur's reaction to the tip?

   A Indifference.
   B Subservience.
   C Affection.
   D Gratitude.

38 The people Guy saw

   A were all physically similar.
   B were extremely varied physically.
   C varied enormously in the way they dressed.
   D were all dressed in the same way.

39 Which of these issues did Guy think about?

   A Race discrimination.
   B The environment.
   C Sexism.
   D Inequality of wealth.

40 The style of the text indicates that it is taken from

   A a novel.
   B a tourist brochure.
   C a news report.
   D a conversation between friends.

PAPER 2 COMPOSITION 2 hours

*Write **two only** of the following composition exercises. Your answers must follow exactly the instructions given. Write in pen, not pencil. You are allowed to make alterations, but make sure your work is clear and easy to read.*

1   Describe your favourite month or season of the year. (About 350 words)

2   Which do you think is the transport system of the future: road or rail? (About 350 words)

3   Write a story which begins with the words: 'I switched on the TV news and . . .' (About 350 words)

4   Write a letter in reply to this advertisement from a student magazine. (About 350 words)

> **YOUNG HORIZONS** is a charitable organisation which specialises in advising youth clubs on locations abroad. If your town has something to offer small groups of English-speaking visitors, please let us have details on all the sports and leisure facilities in the area, and we'll get in touch with you – wherever you may be. Letters to: Cathy, Young Horizons, 15, Park Road East, Nottingham N12 5PB.

5   Set books.

PAPER 3 USE OF ENGLISH 2 hours

SECTION A

1 *Fill each of the numbered blanks in the passage with **one** suitable word.*

A team led by Dr Michael Levi, reader in criminology, has completed a year-long study of assaults on police. The findings, as _____ (1) unpublished, show that fears of assault and the influence of alcohol in attacks are greatly exaggerated _____ (2) the police and that newspaper _____ (3) tends, in general, to be alarmist. _____ (4) statistics for assaults on police have only been collected since 1990, Dr Levi says there is no hard _____ (5) that violence was very much less in the past. A golden _____ (6) when violence against the police was virtually unknown _____ (7) existed. _____ (8), the modern officer does _____ (9) to endure a large number of insults, which fuel a perception _____ (10) officers that they are _____ (11) threat and _____ (12) in widespread contempt.

The research did recommend a number of _____ (13) police forces _____ (14) adopt to lessen the risk of attack. _____ (15) is to stop overtime shifts _____ (16) weekends, when officers are tired and policing is therefore less effective. Officers should also be more careful _____ (17) the way they approach the public. 'It was the way he spoke to me,' was a common reason _____ (18) by assailants interviewed. Police officers should _____ (19) standing too close because it 'winds people _____ (20)' and interviewees feel threatened.

2 *Finish each of the following sentences in such a way that it is as similar as possible in meaning to the sentence printed before it.*

Example: He always finds time to lend a hand.
Answer: He's never *too busy to lend a hand.*

a We cannot deny that serious mistakes have been made.

   There is _____

b It is vital that people see that the system is changing.

   The system must be _____

c They pointed a gun at the manager and forced him to open the safe.

   The manager was _____

d There has been universal condemnation of their threat to kill hostages.

   Their threat _____

e Observers believe he resigned because of financial irregularities.

He is _____

f The two wings of the Party are deeply divided.

There is _____

g If they hadn't warned us, we'd have made exactly the same mistake.

If it _____

h We very much regret the closure, although there really was no alternative.

Much _____

3 *Fill each of the blanks with a suitable word or phrase.*

Example: The doctor said I should ____*take it*____ easy for a while.

a While we're out, help _____ any eats and drinks you fancy.

b In such a delicate situation, the least _____ better.

c He is very clever _____ talking people into doing things.

d What a nasty thing to do! You _____ of yourself.

e Eventually he was found, suffering from frostbite _____ around for days in the Arctic conditions.

f I wouldn't go so _____ say he's a liar, but he certainly tends to exaggerate a bit.

4 *For each of the sentences below, write a new sentence as similar as possible in meaning to the original sentence, but using the word given. This word **must not be altered** in any way.*

Example: When are you going to find time to decorate the kitchen?
      round
Answer: *When are you going to get round to decorating the kitchen?*

a The police fired and several people were killed.
dead

_____

b Why don't we hire a rowing boat for an hour?
about

_____

c Given a good start, I'm sure she'll win.
provided

_____

d The value of the country's exports went up sharply last month.
upturn

_____

e   The original plan has been extensively modified.
    modifications

_____

f   Before they gained promotion, attendances were a third of what they are now.
    trebled

_____

g   The accusation that he had stolen the money was unfounded.
    wrongly

_____

h   Who else was this information available to?
    access

_____

SECTION B

5 *Read the following passage, then answer the questions which follow it.*

I went fire walking the other day. This is not a joke. I stood in front of a 12-foot bed of red-hot charcoal and walked the length in my bare feet which, at the end, tingled slightly. As you might imagine.

The call to apparent self-immolation came from Michael Hutchinson, who's the British representative of the *Skeptical Inquirer*, the American magazine which uses investigation and   5
science to counter paranormal claims such as telepathy, spoon-bending, spiritualism and allied claptrap. Recently the skeptics (they prefer the US spelling) have been getting agitated about fraudulent seminars where people are told that their minds will be given mastery over their bodies – for a large fee, of course. The climax of each session is a fire walk. Naturally, the people who do it are astounded and tend to believe that they performed a miracle, for which $350 seems   10
remarkably cheap. So the Wessex Skeptics decided they would prove that there's nothing miraculous about it.

Fire walking is possible for several reasons; it depends partly on the heat capacity of the burning material, partly on its thermal conductivity, the speed at which it passes heat into anything that touches it. Think of an oven heated to, say, 225 centigrade. You can put your hand in quite easily.   15
You can even touch the roast meat without suffering more than a momentary twinge. But if your finger brushes the metal rack – which is at exactly the same temperature – you're in agony for hours. In the same way, anyone who tried fire walking across aluminium would quickly find they had no feet. But wood has a very low thermal conductivity. By the time the burning charcoal realises your foot is there, it isn't any more (though sappy wood, like pine, is horribly dangerous,   20
since it can stick to your foot). Fire walkers in places like Fiji prefer glowing pumice, which looks terrific but has such low thermal conductivity that you could perform the carioca on it. Well, almost.

The fire was ready. It was too hot to put your hand within a few inches, and a steak would have needed 30 seconds each side at most. First came Robin Allen. He looked worried. There was a   25
certain amount of what would be regular, fire walkers' 'guy' talk, if anyone fire walked regularly. 'Will somebody tell me again why we're doing this thing?' he asked. Then he took a deep breath, walked briskly across, slipped into the tray of water at the far end, and fell flat on his backside. Luckily the tray skidded so that he didn't land in the coals. Next came the others who'd done it before. They reported that it felt warm, but no worse than hot sand on a beach. Then the   30
amateurs, led by Michael, who was splendid: calm, no fuss at all.

Suddenly I realised it was my turn. This was a problem. I applied philosophy to it. Either it was as easy as it looked, or else the others had sprayed asbestos on their feet and the whole event was a cruel joke at my expense. Occam's razor (which means in effect that the simplest explanation is probably true) caused me to reject the latter possibility. Therefore there was no reason why I   35 should not go. Except for stark, utter terror. We spend a lifetime being conditioned to avoid contact with fire. All the scientific logic in the world, even the evidence of your eyes, can't remove the basic imprint. And that fire was *hot*.

In the end, I went for the most banal of reasons. They'd opened another six-pack at the other end, and were drinking to their success. Fear had made my mouth dry. I needed that beer. If it   40
meant strolling barefoot across a four-yard inferno, so be it. Yes, it prickled slightly, and I was glad it wasn't 24 foot long. I was also glad to have watched the others' gait: toes up out of the fire, otherwise flat-footed so that the pressure is soft and even. I think I took only four, perhaps five steps. Then the joy of the cold soggy blanket waiting at the end. And the beer, the best I've ever tasted.   45

a   Give another expression for 'allied claptrap' (line 6).

_____

_____

b   What, according to the writer, is the motive of the seminar organisers, and why should $350 seem 'remarkably cheap' (line 11)?

_____

_____

_____

c   What does the example of the oven demonstrate?

_____

_____

d   Explain the difference between charcoal and pine wood from the point of view of a fire walker.

_____

_____

e   What do you think the 'carioca' (line 22) is, and what point is the writer making when he says "Well, almost."?

_____

_____

f   What is the purpose of the reference on line 24 to 'a steak'?

_____

_____

g   Explain what the passage says about "regular, fire walkers' 'guy' talk" (line 26)

_____

_____

h What went wrong during the first fire walker's crossing?

_____

_____

_____

i What was it that 'the others had done' (line 29) 'before'?

_____

_____

j How did the writer decide it was logical that he would not get burnt?

_____

_____

k Why was he so frightened?

_____

_____

l Why did he finally walk across the coals?

_____

_____

m Explain the phrase 'so be it' (line 41).

_____

_____

n What advantage did the writer have over the other firewalkers?

_____

_____

o In a paragraph of 70–90 words, state the reasons why the skeptics went firewalking and explain why it is not as dangerous as it might seem.

_____

_____

_____

_____

_____

_____

_____

_____

PAPER 4 LISTENING COMPREHENSION about 30 minutes

FIRST PART

For question 1 you should fill in the missing details. You are given an example of what to write.

1

    a Type of aircraft *Boeing 737*

    b Landing cards not required for citizens of the _____

    c Air traffic control restrictions during the _____

    d Aeroplane has come from _____

    e Destination of flight _____

    f Duration of flight _____

    g Flying altitude _____

    h Landing conditions _____

    i Details of life jackets on a _____

    j Total number of emergency exits _____

    k On escape slide, do not wear _____

SECOND PART

For questions 2–6 tick one of the boxes A, B, C or D.

2 The first speaker thinks that Guns 'n' Roses

    A cannot play music.

    B perform better than they compose.

    C should be discussed.

    D create better music than classical composers.

A	
B	
C	
D	

3 ''I think it's quite possible they've never done anything else''. The tone of this remark implies

    A astonishment.

    B praise.

    C criticism.

    D disinterest.

A	
B	
C	
D	

4 When Bill says ''Thanks a lot Paul'' he sounds

    A sarcastic.

    B grateful.

    C miserable.

    D reassured.

A	
B	
C	
D	

5 How many of the speakers are against rock being studied at school?

    A None.

    B One.

    C Two.

    D Three.

A	
B	
C	
D	

6 Throughout this extract, the presenter tries to

    A avoid the discussion going on too long.

    B ensure that his own opinions prevail.

    C broaden the subject under discussion.

    D provoke arguments amongst the speakers.

A	
B	
C	
D	

THIRD PART

7 *For question **7** tick whether you think the statements are **true** or **false**.*

    a The 'parasol' idea would be very cheap.

    b Dr Broecker says we should make volcanoes erupt more often.

    c Polystyrene could be used to lower the Earth's temperature.

    d We could dump liquid carbon dioxide.

    e We could feed marine plant life.

    f Jaques suggests farming algae in the middle of the North Sea.

    g Wood might once again become a major energy source.

    h There is a new wood-fired power station in Central America.

True	False

FOURTH PART

*For questions **8–12** tick one of the boxes **A**, **B**, **C** or **D**.*

8   The speaker mentions *The Greedy and Lazy Illiterate's Way to a Publishing Fortune*

   A   as an example of negative thinking.

   B   to parody self-help books.

   C   to promote his own book.

   D   as an example of a book that failed.

A	
B	
C	
D	

9   According to the speaker, the title should

   A   take half a minute to read.

   B   make exaggerated claims.

   C   tell the truth.

   D   be no longer than three words.

A	
B	
C	
D	

10   The shorter the self-help book,

   A   the quicker the method seems to be.

   B   the slimmer the reader will become.

   C   the less money the writer will make.

   D   the fewer the ideas can be included.

A	
B	
C	
D	

11   You should write about how to

   A   lose weight.

   B   deal with stress.

   C   cope with divorce.

   D   find a wife.

A	
B	
C	
D	

12   The speaker's tone throughout is

   A   bullying.

   B   gloomy.

   C   puzzled.

   D   light hearted.

A	
B	
C	
D	

PAPER 5 INTERVIEW

The theme of this Test is **Speed**.

1 a Look at *one* of the photographs and describe:
□ the setting
□ the people and the objects
□ what the people are probably going to do

If you are doing the interview in a group, contrast the people in your photograph with those in the others'.

b Now discuss:
□ the sub-culture associated with the activity in the picture
□ the reasons why young people find speed so exciting
□ its dangers

2   Study *one* of these passages. You may quote from it if you wish.

a   Is there really much point in developing a Mach 25 space plane at a cost estimated at over £8 billion before the first flight? Even if all the technological difficulties – the enormous temperatures, the flexing of the fuselage in flight, the tremendous velocity of the air entering the engines and so on – can be overcome, no-one has the slightest idea what the operating costs would be: commercial success is far from guaranteed.

b   OK now, make sure you get a quick take-off: it's a bit blowy today. Once you're up there you're on your own. Keep well away from those rocks, remember your gliding 'chute is taking you forward much faster than would an ordinary one. And don't forget to have your skis ready at the right . . . at the correct angle as I showed you so you don't get all panicky over the last couple of metres if you're not quite sure what height you're at: what we call 'ground rush'. Right, off you go.

c   Even in that most gentlemanly of sports, yacht racing, competitors have now been caught cheating in an attempt to go faster. Some have secretly been using up to 200kg more ballast than the rules allow in events such as the Admiral's Cup, jettisoning the containers before the yachts are checked at the end of the race. Moving the extra ballast weight is like having an extra 3 crew members, whose numbers are also restricted, changing position on board.

Where do you think the text is taken from?
Who do you think the speaker or writer might be?
What is the purpose of the text?
Discuss the content.

3   Do *one* of these tasks.

a   Give your views on this statement:
'Modern-day society's obsession with speed is one of the biggest causes of harm to the environment.'
You can be for or against the proposal. You may like to think about the following points when preparing your speech:
☐   the over-use of scarce energy resources
☐   greater pollution at high speed
☐   the damage to the countryside: new motorways, airports, railways etc.
☐   faster routes may generate more traffic.

b   Look at the advertisement
How would you use the service offered?
What are its limitations?
What social and environmental criticisms could be made of it?

London Gatwick's Largest Executive Jet Operator

INTERFLIGHT

★ Lear Jet 500mph + For 2,200 Miles
★ Hawker 125 Mini Airliner With First Class Hostess Service
★ Choose Your Own Timetable To Optimise Your Business Potential
★ We Offer A 24 Hour Service For Those Last Minute Urgent Flights

Discuss Your Own Personal Charter Requirements With Melanie Mair On 0293 540409

CHARTERING IS EASIER THAN YOU THINK!

Interflight Aircharter Ltd, 76A The Beehive, Gatwick Airport, RH6 0LA

TEST THREE

SECTION A

In this section you must choose the word or phrase which best completes each sentence. **On your answer sheet** *indicate the letter* **A**, **B**, **C** *or* **D** *against the number of each item 1 to 25 for the word or phrase you choose.*

1 After years of discrimination and harrassment they are at last beginning to fight _____ .

   A against   **B** back   **C** on   **D** off

2 They took _____ of her kindness and stole everything she had.

   A advantage   **B** profit   **C** abuse   **D** benefit

3 Until the storm dies down _____ we can do is hope.

   A everything   **B** only   **C** all   **D** nothing

4 The critics loved it but myself I thought it was a _____ of rubbish.

   A stack   **B** pile   **C** load   **D** lot

5 It will take time to put the plan _____ effect.

   A into   **B** in   **C** on   **D** onto

6 Covering the wound with a plaster would probably do more _____ than good.

   A hurt   **B** bad   **C** ill   **D** harm

7 The governor called on the prisoners to give themselves _____ or else the jail would be stormed.

   A in   **B** up   **C** over   **D** out

8 We're quite happy with the service as it is, but I _____ the council will change it before long.

   A expect   **B** wish   **C** hope   **D** wait

9 The unseasonally high temperatures have made it one of the _____ winters on record.

   A softest   **B** mildest   **C** weakest   **D** meekest

10 It was one of the most _____ fought matches of the tournament.

   A keenly   **B** pointedly   **C** sharply   **D** finely

11 On her return home, she gave an exciting _____ of her adventures.

   A story   **B** tale   **C** account   **D** history

12 It's not the only reason, but we bought it _____ because of the colour.

   A somewhat   **B** partly   **C** almost   **D** extensively

13 When the two of them get together, they'll be a force to be _____ with.

   A frightened   **B** handled   **C** reckoned   **D** faced

14 When the ten minutes are _____ a bell will ring.

   A out   **B** off   **C** up   **D** down

15 The authorities warned _____ immigrants that even fewer entry visas were available.

A would-be **B** going-over **C** has-been **D** have-nots

16 The council are to set _____ a committee to look into the problem.

A up **B** out **C** in **D** off

17 Several ministers were _____ in the cabinet reshuffle.

A fallen **C** dropped **C** terminated **D** resigned

18 In the raids which followed, police _____ drugs with a street value of over £10 million.

A held **B** seized **C** took **D** detained

19 First reports _____ the explosion on a gas leak.

A blame **B** attribute **C** accuse **D** inform

20 He was _____ the first to use the technique, but he is probably the best-known.

A on no account **B** in no doubt **C** by no means **D** less than sure

21 It was _____ to the point where people needed hospital treatment.

A reaching **B** getting **C** arriving **D** going

22 Our main _____ is with the many victims of the tragedy.

A concern **B** worry **C** interest **D** anxiety

23 It's not _____ who actually painted it.

A sure **B** certain **C** safe **D** positive

24 This is by far the best party _____ for years.

A I've been to **B** I was at **C** I'm at **D** I went to

25 They're supposed to be well past their best but _____ we went to see them play.

A no matter what **B** all the same **C** even if **D** without any doubt

SECTION B

*In this section you will find after each of the passages a number of questions or unfinished statements about the passage, each with four suggested answers or ways of finishing. You must choose the one which you think fits best according to the passage. **On your answer sheet**, indicate the letter **A**, **B**, **C** or **D** against the number of each item **26** to **40** for the answer you choose. Give **one answer only** to each question. Read each passage right through before choosing your answers.*

FIRST PASSAGE

Friday, 30 November 1849. 'Well, Ephraim,' said Marshal Tukey to the janitor, 'was it the turkey Mr Webster gave you that made you so suspicious?'

'I should say not, sir,' Littlefield replied, not meeting the Marshal's steady gaze. 'It were well before that, on Sunday, that I thought I should watch the Professor, and I told the wife I'd do it, even though she was none too happy about such a snooping and a prying.'

'But the turkey, Ephraim,' the Marshal insisted with a kind of serious merriment not appropriate to the moment, 'did you eat it, then, you and Mrs Littlefield?'

'Wouldn't it have been a sin to waste it, with us making the holiday on the pretty little the college pays us?'

'And was it a good bird, the Professor's turkey?'

'Good enough.' The janitor had always been uneasy in the presence of the Marshal. Tukey had a way of looking so hard and direct at you out of those grey eyes that you didn't know what he was up to.

'So on Thanksgiving you had your dinner and then set to work to find the body?'

'I were mighty tired of all the talk, wherever I went, in the market and the Lodge, as to how if they were to find the Doctor it would be in the Medical College, and all those queer looks coming my way as if I had something to do with the business. I reckoned seeing as how your men had been through the place, all that was left was the privy vault, and if nothing was there, that would be the end of it.'

'But you thought there might be something there, didn't you Ephraim?'

'I don't know what I thought, sir. I wanted to be done with it, I know that.'

'And the reward, Mr Littlefield,' Tukey asked, shifting to a less familiar form of address, 'assuming that what we have are the remains of the Doctor, will you be collecting the reward posted by the Doctor's brother-in-law, Mr Shaw?'

'Have I ever said I would, Mr Tukey?' the janitor replied, with a note of anger sharpening the edge of his low voice, yet not quite answering the question. A long moment of embarrassed silence followed. Why, with all that had happened this day and him still a-trembling with it all, was he the one to get such questions as these? Why should it be he who had to explain himself?

26 At first, Tukey's questioning is

   A lighthearted.

   B remorseless.

   C tentative.

   D impolite.

27 Which phrase shows that Littlefield speaks a dialect of English?

   A she was none too happy

   B a snooping and a prying

   C seeing as how

   D to be done with it

28 Littlefield has

   A already claimed the reward.

   B discussed the case with many people.

   C got a guilty conscience.

   D found evidence of a crime.

29 The janitor suspects

   A Mrs Littlefield.

   B the Professor.

   C Shaw.

   D the Doctor.

30 Towards the end of the dialogue, Tukey's tone becomes more

   A blunt.

   B formal.

   C colloquial.

   D affable.

SECOND PASSAGE

The term 'sleepwalking' may be a misnomer, according to a research report. Sufferers from this distressing condition may in fact be awake, but in a 'dissociated' state of mind. Professor Arthur Crisp describes dissociation as a breakdown in the normal integration of the mind, when a small group of mental processes can, in effect, take over. He says that dissociation is a defensive mechanism, which seems to block out feelings of distress.

On most aspects of personality, people who walk in their sleep seem no different from anyone else. But sleep walkers score very highly on certain specific measures – it seems they particularly enjoy dramatic situations, acting, or being the centre of attention. These traits are also strong in patients who suffer from 'night terrors' – the tendency to wake suddenly from deep, non-dreaming, sleep in a state of panic.

The researchers believe that both sleepwalking and night terrors are linked to similar traits present in sufferers' waking personalities. But they point out that the differences in personality profiles between their patients and the general population are very specific, and not related to a general mental disorder; patients with neurotic or psychotic problems typically differ from the norm for a wide range of personality measures.

But what makes some people sleepwalkers, and others suffer from night terrors? The difference, the researchers suggest, is that a typical sleepwalker scores slightly higher than usual for measures of hostility. Night terror sufferers, on the other hand, tend to be worriers, with higher measures for anxiety.

The team liken the sleepwalker's state of mind to the temporary disorientation felt by most of us, if we are woken suddenly. But among sleepwalkers, sudden waking may be common, and disorientation extends into dissociation.

Understanding the factors underlying sleepwalking is vital if doctors are to help sufferers, who sometimes injure themselves, and may disturb the sleep of their partners.

But the issue also has legal repercussions. In rare instances, sleepwalkers can commit acts of violence, and even murder. In extreme cases, sufferers have resorted to tying themselves to their beds, for fear of their actions. A problem, in these sad cases, is the extent to which sleepwalkers can be held legally responsible for their actions.

Professor Crisp hopes that his research will contribute to the debate. Sleepwalking behaviour may be linked to real traits in sufferers' personalities, but these may only be expressed during dissociation, when 'normal' control of the mind seems to have broken down. If Crisp's interpretation of sleepwalking is correct, lawyers and forensic psychiatrists face a difficult problem.

31 Professor Crisp claims that dissociation

    A seems to occur when a person is asleep.
    B is the result of a relaxed state of mind.
    C only happens during the night.
    D apparently has a calming effect.

32 According to the text, sleepwalkers

    A have completely different characters from sufferers of night terrors.
    B are suffering from a serious mental illness.
    C should never be woken up suddenly.
    D at first react like non-sleepwalkers when woken suddenly.

33 Sufferers of night terrors

    A often have extrovert personalities.
    B are usually hostile towards other people.
    C worry about their violent behaviour.
    D have particularly unpleasant nightmares.

34 The aim of the research is to

    A improve the treatment for the injuries suffered by sleepwalkers.
    B show sufferers canot be blamed for what they do when sleepwalking.
    C gain knowledge which will improve the treatment for sleepwalking.
    D help the victims of attacks by sleepwalkers.

35 Legal difficulties could arise because

    A many sufferers deny that they sleepwalk.
    B many sufferers have previously had nervous breakdowns.
    C it is hard to get sleepwalkers to undergo treatment.
    D they may actually be awake when sleepwalking.

THIRD PASSAGE

1   Scientists are monitoring the progress of the world's biggest iceberg – 100 miles long and 25 wide – which has broken loose in Antarctica. It could take a decade to work its way into open sea and another three years to break up and melt. 'It's been a bad year.' Dr Chris Sear, a climatologist with the British Antarctic Survey, said. 'There have been 13 others so far.' The 1000-foot-thick iceberg is the second largest recorded since satellite tracking began in the 1960s. The largest, in 1963, was half again as big.

    Scientists are intensely interested in icebergs as the argument continues over whether we are seeing the beginnings of 'the greenhouse effect'. Dr Sear said this iceberg was 'an indication that perhaps there is something going on which maybe we should already be worrying about'.

2   There has been a coalition of interests between scientists who have needed funds and the media who wanted a good story. The common perception of science is of a disinterested pursuit of truth. The reality is rather different. Scientists are no different from any other professional group. In order to pursue their work, they require funding. If you are working in climatology, a good way of attracting interest and backing is to predict an apocalypse.

    Of course, it has not only been the scientists and the media who have promoted the greenhouse theory; politicians have not been slow to see the advantages. What could be less controversial than government action to save Mother Earth?

3   The burgeoning apocalypse industry predicts global warming, pins its cause on rising carbon dioxide levels and pronounces the undiluted disaster of its effect, all as an utter certainty stamped and approved by science. This is false. Scientists agree that there is an accelerating rise in carbon dioxide levels. But they don't know the consequences of the rise and the role other factors may play in warming the atmosphere.

    Moreover, so far from the ice caps melting, recent satellite surveys indicate that the Greenland ice sheet is thickening. The fact is that scientists simply don't know enough to support the wilder predictions now being made. Does this mean the world should do nothing about carbon dioxide emissions? Absolutely not. The risk of unacceptable damage from even a small increase in warming is simply too great to permit inertia.

4   The interesting thing is that this testing of the orthodoxy by its sceptical critics has reassured at least this notorious eco-sceptic that the scientists, eco-freaks and governments have got it about right so far. Certainly, two senior custodians of the concensus talked me through the criticisms point by point this week, and their case seemed undemolished.

    It really does seem likely that man has already set in train dangerous and unpredictable changes in the world's climate because of his emissions of carbon dioxide, methane, various CFCs and a ragbag of other gases. It is likely that nothing on earth can stop some uncomfortable effects of emissions made earlier this century, and the issue looks likely to become one of how far to go to stop the effect becoming worse.

36 Which is fact, not opinion?

   A Extract 1
   B Extract 2
   C Extract 3
   D Extract 4

37 How many extracts predict alarming new weather patterns?

   A One
   B Two
   C Three
   D Four

38 How many extracts suggest we should ignore warnings of climatic change?

   A One
   B Two
   C Three
   D Four

39 How many extracts contain arguments both for and against the existence of global warming?

   A One
   B Two
   C Three
   D Four

40 Which is the most cynical?

   A Extract 1
   B Extract 2
   C Extract 3
   D Extract 4

PAPER 2 COMPOSITION 2 hours

*Write **two only** of the following composition exercises. Your answers must follow exactly the instructions given. Write in pen, not pencil. You are allowed to make alterations, but make sure your work is clear and easy to read.*

1 Describe the work of a charity which you admire. (About 350 words)

2 'There should be one world language.' Discuss. (About 350 words)

3 Tell the story of an oppressed group of people's struggle for freedom. (About 350 words)

4 The town council is proposing the measures referred to below. Write a letter to a friend explaining what is happening and suggesting alternative ways of saving money. (About 300 words)

PUBLIC ANNOUNCEMENT

On account of the prevailing economic circumstances, substantial reductions in Local Authority expenditure will be necessary.

The above will entail the following modifications:

— No further school or hospital building projects will be undertaken.
— Sports centres will henceforth open at weekends only.

BUS SERVICES TO BE CUT

Sir,
We wish to express, in the strongest possible terms, our total opposition to the planned suspension of library facilities in the district of

---

Sir,
Our attention has been drawn to the projected reduction in the frequency of refuse collection and street cleaning in this borough. We feel

---

Social Services: Job Losses

---

5 Set books.

PAPER 3 USE OF ENGLISH 2 hours

SECTION A

1 *Fill each of the numbered blanks in the passage with **one** suitable word.*

Consider the environmental and social benefits of an efficient railway system. It is illogical that the

railways _____ (1) be required to show an eight per cent return on investment, while no

_____ (2) return _____ (3) or can be expected from roads – except on the basis

_____ (4) cost benefit analysis. _____ (5) is the rough tool used to assess the

notional benefits brought by road construction. It has never been applied by the Department of

Transport to investment _____ (6) the railway system. Roads are built _____ (7)

taxpayers' money and create much pollution and other damage. They produce no profit

_____ (8) such. Why should railways, which are less destructive, and safer, have to

_____ (9) so?

   Applying cost benefit analysis to the railways' services would bring home _____ (10) the

Government the profound social and economic value of a first-class national railway network.

Among items on the credit _____ (11) of the balance sheet would be a _____ (12)

in pollution by road users, less death and injury _____ (13) the roads, a saving of the time

_____ (14) in traffic jams, and a more efficient use of energy than _____ (15) of

short-haul aircraft and road vehicles. All these can be quantified, _____ (16) many of them

are quantified when _____ (17) whether and where to build roads.

   How different many decisions _____ (18) the closure of loss-making branch lines

_____ (19) have been if such factors had been taken into _____ (20).

2 *Finish each of the following sentences in such a way that it is as similar as possible in meaning to the sentence printed before it.*

   Example: He was careful to behave extremely well.
   Answer: He was on *his best behaviour.*

   a He wasn't offered the job because he couldn't provide references.

      If _____

   b She gave him a friendly smile as she left.

      She smiled _____

   c His plan shows little business sense or concern for the environment.

      His plan shows as _____

d We'd have missed the flight if we hadn't set out early.

It's just as _____

e He's so competitive that he never gives up.

He's too much _____

f The management were threatened with strike action when they laid off some of the workers.

On _____

g In future, employers will have to comply with the law.

No longer _____

h After the meeting, all the leaders present refused to comment.

None _____

3 *Fill each of the blanks with a suitable word or phrase.*

Example: They came through the doors two ____*at a*____ time.

a They were on the point _____ up when a sudden breakthrough encouraged them to persevere.

b The Prime Minister denied being _____ touch with ordinary people's feelings.

c I really don't care whether they win or lose; it's all _____ me.

d Into view _____ a scene of unimaginable beauty.

e The management reserve _____ refuse admission.

f He reached across the table but, _____ doing, spilt the water.

g Barely _____ to repair the damage when a second earthquake struck the town.

4 *For each of the sentences below, write a new sentence as similar as possible in meaning to the original sentence, but using the word given. This word **must not be altered** in any way.*

Example: The escaped prisoner has still not been caught.
        large
Answer: *The escaped prisoner is still at large.*

a The exam results will come out in September.
passed

_____

b Call us the moment you get there.
first

_____

c I really didn't like the look of the food in that place.
appeal

_____

d It was time to make a fresh start.
come

_____

e Less than half the present amount is going to be spent on defence.
cut

_____

f It has gone more or less according to plan so far.
wrong

_____

g She'll probably win the case.
chances

_____

h Nobody had to ask her to put her toys away when she'd finished playing.
accord

_____

SECTION B

5 *Read the following passage, then answer the questions which follow it.*

What makes someone confess to a crime committed by somebody else? It seems so unnatural that we may discount the possibility. When a case does arise, we are inclined to regard it as exceptional, and proof that the confessors must have been put under extreme physical and psychological pressure. We may be able to imagine admitting a minor crime such as shoplifting to escape a police interrogation, but we find it much harder to believe that an innocent person would confess to a   5
serious offence like murder.

But most well-publicised serious crimes spawn a crop of eccentrics who 'confess' to them, perhaps because of a desire for publicity or because of fantasies about committing the crime – over 200 people 'confessed' to the kidnapping in 1932 of the two-year-old son of the American aviator Charles Lindbergh. The police often keep some details of a serious crime secret to enable them to   10
screen out such people.

More important to the criminal justice system, and harder for the police to spot, are two other kinds of false confession resulting from interrogation. In the first type, the 'coerced compliant' confession, a person knows he or she hasn't committed the crime but confesses to gain some immediate benefit – like being released from custody. Sometimes such people think they will be   15
able to establish the truth later on. But in the other type of case, the 'coerced internalised' confession, a suspect becomes at least temporarily persuaded that he or she might have, or did, commit the crime, and begins to accept suggestions offered by the police.

Dr Gisli Gudjonsson, a psychologist, and Dr James MacKeith, a psychiatrist, have examined the psychological backdrop to the false confession. Dr Gudjonsson has studied nearly 150 cases in   20
which confessions were retracted. Two psychological qualities appear to be involved: 'interrogative suggestibility' and 'compliance'. Interrogative suggestibility is the tendency to accept, uncritically, information communicated during questioning: compliance is the tendency to do what you are told. Highly suggestible people are more likely to make coerced internalised confessions. Compliant people are more likely to make compliant confessions.   25

Dr Gudjonsson, a former police detective in Iceland, has devised a method of measuring suggestibility. His test is becoming part of the forensic psychologist's armoury. In one experiment he examined 12 people who had confessed to crimes but later retracted. He called this group the 'false confessors'. He compared them with eight people who had been charged with crimes but persistently denied them in spite of evidence – the 'deniers'. He found that on a scale of one to 15,   30
the false confessors had an average suggestibility score of 10.5, while the deniers averaged three. The deniers were four points below the score for normal males, suggesting that they were remarkably strong-minded individuals.

But not all the 'false confessors' had high suggestibility scores. This is not entirely surprising, since some of the retracted confessions may actually have been genuine. Or there may have been   35 other psychological factors at work – such as compliance. According to Dr Gudjonsson, compliance is linked to a general willingness to please and a desire to avoid the unpleasant consequences of not complying. It is difficult to measure experimentally, but can be gauged by asking people to fill in questionnaires about themselves. Guilty feelings, he says, are an important element of compliance. 'If you want to get people to do things that they don't want to do, then 40 inducing guilt is a very powerful tactic. Let's say I want you to participate in an experiment, but you don't want to do it because it will take a long time. The fact that I have spent time talking to you would facilitate that process, because if you said "no" you might feel guilty. I've certainly seen cases where guilt has been manipulated in police interviews. It may not be that common, but I have seen it.' 45

Gudjonsson and MacKeith's work is bedevilled by the fact that in very few cases of retracted confessions is it possible to establish the 'ground truth' – what *really* happened. The fact that someone has been acquitted of a crime to which he or she confessed is not conclusive – it may have been on a technicality. Conversely, there are cases where almost everyone agrees that there has been a miscarriage of justice. 50

2 **a** Explain the use of 'does' (line 2) in this context.

_____

_____

b Give another expression for 'spawn a crop of eccentrics' (line 7).

_____

c Why did so many people claim they had kidnapped Lindbergh's son?

_____

_____

d What does 'screen out such people' (line 11) mean?

_____

_____

e Why do people make 'coerced compliant' (line 13) confessions and what risk might some of them be running?

_____

_____

_____

f What is the most important difference between the 'coerced internalised' confession and the 'coerced compliant'?

_____

_____

g Who gives the 'information' referred to on line 23 and what is implied about it?

_____

_____

h What sort of confessors actually believe they committed the crime?

_____

_____

i Explain what is meant in this context by 'armoury' (line 27).

_____

j Who or what were the 'deniers' (line 30)?

_____

_____

k What kind of 'false confessor' might be expected to be ''strong-minded''?

_____

_____

l Explain how psychologists test people for 'compliance' (line 36).

_____

_____

m What is meant by the phrase 'on a technicality' (line 49)?

_____

_____

n How would a 'miscarriage of justice' (line 50) affect the confessor and the researchers?

_____

_____

o In a paragraph of 70–90 words, summarise the reasons why people make false confessions.

_____

_____

_____

_____

_____

_____

_____

_____

_____

_____

PAPER 4   LISTENING COMPREHENSION   about 30 minutes

FIRST PART

*For questions 1–5, tick **one** of the boxes A, B, C or D.*

1   Jenny thinks unpunctual people

    A   are responsible for many homicides.

    B   steal other people's time.

    C   deserve our sympathy.

    D   ruined her father's business.

A	
B	
C	
D	

2   When she says *Really?*, the Presenter sounds

    A   amused.

    B   shocked.

    C   bored.

    D   patronising.

A	
B	
C	
D	

3   According to Jenny, Sticklers

    A   always remain calm, whatever the situation.

    B   fear that people will not wait for them.

    C   often have very arrogant personalities.

    D   are obsessed with clocks and watches.

A	
B	
C	
D	

4   She believes that Amblers

    A   spend a lot of time waiting for other people.

    B   enjoy making other people suffer.

    C   are too lazy to do any housework.

    D   do not realise how much trouble they cause.

A	
B	
C	
D	

5   Jenny is probably

    A   punctual, with a punctual partner.

    B   unpunctual, with a punctual partner.

    C   punctual, with an unpunctual partner.

    D   unpunctual, with an unpunctual partner.

A	
B	
C	
D	

SECOND PART

For questions 6–11 fill in the correct answer.

Make of video: **6** _____

Model: **7** _____

Already checked
By Jeff: **8** _____

9 _____

10 _____

Video channel no.: **11** _____

For questions 12 and 13 tick one of the boxes A, B, C or D.

12 Why did Jeff ring?

  A To find out how the speaker was.

  B To ask for advice.

  C To give the speaker some information.

  D To ask the speaker to lend him something.

A	
B	
C	
D	

13 The speaker feels that Jeff

  A hasn't looked after the video properly.

  B should speak to a real expert.

  C is being rather uncooperative.

  D bought a poor quality video.

A	
B	
C	
D	

THIRD PART

14 *For question **14** tick whether you think the statements are **true** or **false**.*

		True	False
a	The four categories apply only to women in the UK.		
b	'Stay-at-home' women are usually well-educated.		
c	'Just-a-job' women are currently working.		
d	Most American women stay at home.		
e	Statistics on the proportion of women who work in the UK are unreliable.		
f	Far more housewives prefer to stay at home in Britain than in Brazil.		
g	In nearly all the countries, most working women regard their jobs as careers.		
h	The smallest change will probably be in Germany.		
i	British women are more interested in having children than a career.		
j	Relatively few Japanese women have children.		

FOURTH PART

*For questions 15–19 tick **one** of the boxes **A**, **B**, **C** or **D**.*

15 Tenosynovitis

    A causes an intermittent pain.

    B can only be treated by surgery.

    C is caused by working with one's hands.

    D has only recently been identified.

A	
B	
C	
D	

16 Specific causes include

    A cooking meals.

    B using computers.

    C doing the shopping.

    D drinking alcohol.

A	
B	
C	
D	

17 The condition is controversial because

    A little compensation is paid to sufferers.

    B it might be less common than is often thought.

    C it might not really exist at all.

    D sufferers tend to overstate the pain it causes.

A	
B	
C	
D	

18 Which of these have the most to gain financially from denying that tenosynovitis is the cause?

    A Patients.

    B Trade unions.

    C Bosses.

    D Doctors.

A	
B	
C	
D	

19 Pell says the condition is due to

    A physical factors only.

    B the nature of present-day work.

    C psychological factors only.

    D pressure from doctors and lawyers.

A	
B	
C	
D	

PAPER 5 INTERVIEW

The theme of this Test is **Students**.

1 **a** Look at *one* of the photographs and describe:
  ☐ the setting
  ☐ the people
  ☐ the likely atmosphere

  If you are doing the interview in a group, contrast your picture with the others'.

  b Now discuss:
  ☐ the accusation that universities are elitist
  ☐ alternatives to university
  ☐ the higher education system in your country

2   Study *one* of these passages. You may quote from it if you wish.

a   Yeah we really thought we were going to change it all by er saying it with cobblestones – that was it – cause it seemed it was happening all over the place and there was so much energy and creativity but somehow it all fizzled out like in that song; maybe because the workers here thought we were just a bunch of clowns – not like in France – and also because in the States once the risk of getting drafted er off to Vietnam had gone you kind of got the feeling that that people were losing interest.

b   The Council of Europe has recently drawn up a list of over 160 British organisations which offer completely worthless qualifications in exchange for a CV and a fee: £900 will buy a BA and a £1500 doctorate from places with impressive-sounding names but no academic recognition whatsoever. Many of these bogus universities advertise abroad and it is often difficult for potential 'graduates' as well as prospective employers, to identify them. Hence the Council's list.

c   We inherit from the Renaissance the idea of a liberal education, originally based upon the classics. This is supposed to produce the 'whole man'. Beyond this ideal of wholeness university education was not thought to have a particular 'purpose'. Even an apparently vocational subject like law was taught in an academic way, with students having to acquire at least a smattering of Roman law. The current opinion is that this nefarious ideal has seduced generations of the young, and stifled the entrepreneurial spirit of the nation.

Where do you think the text is taken from?
Who do you think the speaker or writer might be?
What is the purpose of the text?
Discuss the content.

3   Do *one* of these tasks.

a   Give your opinion on this statement:
'Students nowadays are not interested in changing society, they just want to make money out of it when they graduate.'

b   Your friend is not sure which subject to study at college or university. Advise him or her, taking into account:
- [ ] the length of the course
- [ ] how difficult it is
- [ ] how interesting it is likely to be
- [ ] its usefulness when looking for a job
- [ ] where the course is available

TEST FOUR

PAPER 1   READING COMPREHENSION   1 hour

SECTION A

In this section you must choose the word or phrase which best completes each sentence. **On your answer sheet** *indicate the letter* **A**, **B**, **C** *or* **D** *against the number of each item 1 to 25 for the word or phrase you choose.*

1 The results were, if _____ C _____ , even better than we had expected.

   A everything   **B** something   **C** anything   **D** nothing

2 Events in the capital have tended to _____ B _____ those elsewhere in the country.

   A overpower   **B** overshadow   **C** oversize   **D** overrule

3 Our position is quite clear; I don't think it needs to be _____ A _____ out.

   A told   **B** spelt   **C** detailed   **D** specified

4 There was an initial mood of optimism at the talks, but now they seem to be making little _____ D _____ .

   A breakthrough   **B** headway   **C** advance   **D** moves

5 With the score at 2–1 the home team seem to have the _____ A _____ hand.

   A upper   **B** stronger   **C** superior   **D** predominant

6 The findings of the enquiry are to be _____ A _____ public in an official report.

   A made   **B** given   **C** shown   **D** explained

7 Government critics poured _____ D _____ on the Minister's appeals for cooperation.

   A contempt   **B** derision   **C** disdain   **D** scorn

8 Take _____ C _____ care not to touch any of the other controls.

   A big   **B** large   **C** great   **D** grand

9 Environmentalists are calling for _____ A _____ laws to combat deforestation.

   A stricter   **B** harder   **C** higher   **D** wider

10 Riot police broke _____ C _____ the demonstration with plastic bullets.

   A down   **B** up   **C** into   **D** off

11 If we're likely to be cut off by snowdrifts, we'd better _____ C _____ up with enough food for a week.

   A build   **B** eat   **C** stock   **D** put

12 Thousands came to _____ D _____ their last respects to the late president.

   A give   **B** mourn   **C** say   **D** pay

13 Suspects may be _____ C _____ without trial for up to two weeks.

   A impounded   **B** locked   **C** held   **D** restrained

14 The two sides _____ D _____ to agree on a workable solution.

   A couldn't   **B** refrained   **C** renounced   **D** failed

15 They now cost twice _____C_____ they did a few years ago.

    A that   **B** which   **C** what   **D** while

16 Victims of the accident are being _____A_____ in local hospitals.

    A treated   **B** cured   **C** healed   **D** operated

17 Samples of the suspect consignment were chosen at _____D_____ for analysis.

    A chance   **B** haphazard   **C** will   **D** random

18 Guerrilla forces _____B_____ an attack on the outskirts of the capital.

    A threw   **B** launched   **C** did   **D** carried

19 It's not _____B_____ the same coming here without the others, is it?

    A rather   **B** quite   **C** fairly   **D** pretty

20 People _____C_____ their savings from banks as rumours of a crisis spread.

    A withheld   **B** retired   **C** withdrew   **D** retreated

21 There's always a massive _____D_____ of holidaymakers in the summer.

    A income   **B** increase   **C** intake   **D** influx

22 The policeman reached for his pistol when he suddenly came _____C_____ with the wanted terrorist.

    A hand-to-hand   **B** ear-to-ear   **C** face-to-face   **D** cheek-to-cheek

23 With the secretary away, everything's in a _____C_____ of utter chaos.

    A stage   **B** position   **C** state   **D** circumstance

24 Please write your name _____A_____ full at the top of the application form.

    A in   **B** out   **C** as   **D** with

25 The job doesn't need finishing until Friday, so take _____B_____ time.

    A much   **B** your   **C** up   **D** this

22/25

SECTION B

In this section you will find after each of the passages a number of questions or unfinished statements about the passage, each with four suggested answers or ways of finishing. You must choose the one which you think fits best according to the passage. **On your answer sheet**, *indicate the letter* **A**, **B**, **C** *or* **D** *against the number of each item 26 to 40 for the answer you choose. Give* **one answer only** *to each question. Read each passage right through before choosing your answers.*

FIRST PASSAGE

I wasn't quite sure how to treat Joel Landais's request to discuss Uropi as a new addition to the European language mountain. After all, there are already about 250 common ways of conversing in the world, plus Esperanto, but Joel has spent the past 15 years developing a vocabulary of 15,000 words. I was worried that he might be a crank even though (or because) he was a regular Guardian reader.

He turned out to be an exceptionally pleasing man with a pretty Spanish wife and a passion for the English way of life developed during student days in Liverpool and recent school exchanges in Crawley, Sussex. As a lycée English teacher who graduated from the Sorbonne, he was obsessed with the idea of doing his bit for European unity, although the roots of Uropi go far beyond the Common Market.

It was originally inspired by reading a dictionary of Indo-European word origins and has become a means of communication based on about 30 per cent Roman, 30 per cent German and 20 per cent Slav among others. The result sounds a bit Saxon, partly because the simplified grammar draws mainly on tidied-up modern English.

In April there will be an exhibition near Paris on the language which Joel taught to a group of linguist friends in about a year and which has been quickly picked up by local secondary school pupils who formed a club to learn Uropi after regular classes.

It takes Joel about four hours to invent a word, basically the common denominator of about 20 European languages. When Uropi is spoken there is an odd impression of just about understanding as in sentences like: 'I vark in a hospital' or 'Bun morna'.

His claims that the language is better balanced and simpler than 19th century Esperanto seemed fair but the main fascination for me was its insight into the formation of European ways of speaking that would overcome the idea that foreign languages were remote from our own.

A couple of years ago Pravda took an interest in Uropi and Joel received 2,000 letters from Russia, particularly from young people who could see it as a short cut to learning the multiple languages we use now. As the average French concierge gets by with only about 800 words from the French Academy's dictionary of 40,000 entries, a foreigner must see a rudimentary uniform European language as a tempting cultural passport.

26 Before he met Landais, the author's attitude to him was

   A   hostile.

   B   sceptical

   C   open-minded.

   D   favourable.

27 On meeting him, the author

   A   felt reassured.

   B   found him very nationalistic.

   C   had his fears confirmed.

   D   thought he was narrowly Western-European.

28 Uropi has been taught in

   A   Spain.

   B   England.

   C   France.

   D   Russia.

29 The author is particularly impressed by the discovery that

   A   Uropi has it origins in so many different languages.

   B   he can understand a certain amount of it.

   C   it is an improvement on Esperanto.

   D   languages could be less of a barrier in the future.

30 People in Russia wrote to Landais because Uropi

   A   might help them learn other languages.

   B   would enable them to converse with ordinary French people.

   C   has 25,000 words fewer than French.

   D   could make it easier for them to get visas.

SECOND PASSAGE

It is bad news for the media on both sides of the Atlantic. Millions of books, television documentaries and newspaper and magazine articles may be put out of date overnight, not to mention dictionaries and word games.

The Rev Jesse Jackson's support for the term 'African-Americans' has led other prominent American black leaders to back it, too. To judge by what happened when 'coloured' was changed to 'negro' and then in the mid-Sixties to 'black', a change to 'African-Americans' now seems inevitable.

As soon as the term becomes official, everything using the word 'black' will thus become dated. You can see the effect in reading the early work of a writer like James Baldwin whose life bridged all the previous changes. His prose is still lively and vivid today, but when he refers to 'negro', it seems old fashioned. Now this will happen with the use of 'black' in contemporary writing and TV programmes.

Jesse Jackson already has formidable backing from black – sorry, African-American – politicians like Ramona Edelin, the National Urban Coalition's president, and some academic departments in the universities already use the term. Jackson claimed that every ethnic group in the US has 'a reference to some land base, some historical cultural base. African-Americans have hit that level of cultural maturity'.

He is right about other ethnic groups in that immigrants who used to describe themselves as merely European, for example, now often identify themselves more closely as Irish Americans, Italian Americans, Polish Americans, Jewish Americans and so on, and have annual parades in the cities displaying their history.

The Rev Willie Barrow, president of Operation Push, the self-help group started by Jesse Jackson in Chicago, said she would start using the term 'African-Americans' immediately. Even some black leaders who thought such concentration on mere names was a sign of what had happened to the civil rights struggle agreed to go along with the change, claiming it would help to raise the consciousness of black Americans and stress their equality with other ethnic groups.

It remains to be seen whether a movement will now start in the US to change the term 'white' which according to Jesse Jackson's argument based on physical appearance and background is just as 'baseless'.

Inevitably, there is already talk about it. This year may become known as the time when both 'black' and 'white' became obsolete.

31 The name 'black'

    A superseded the word ''coloured''.

    B has never been officially recognised.

    C could soon become outmoded.

    D is starting to be used in higher education.

32 James Baldwin

    A now refers to 'African-Americans'.

    B deliberately used offensive words.

    C used the names 'coloured', 'negro' and 'black'.

    D still writes about 'negroes'.

33 The word 'African' would

    A be replaced by names of countries in Africa.

    B be used like 'Irish', 'Italian' etc.

    C show where most US blacks were born.

    D replace the expression 'European'.

34 Some black American leaders

    A identify themselves with other ethnic groups.

    B oppose the change to 'African-Americans'.

    C did not support the civil rights movement.

    D wanted to avoid repeating past mistakes.

35 A campaign against the expression 'white'

    A has already begun.

    B is inevitable.

    C might begin.

    D is inconceivable.

THIRD PASSAGE

In their first years children learn extraordinarily complicated things like walking and talking. At nursery and primary school they mostly show wonderful creativity. And then something goes wrong. According to Marshall McLuhan the reason children don't like going to school is that it interrupts their education.

Personally I quite enjoyed my schooldays but I feel sorry for anyone who says they were the happiest days of their life. I'm sure that many would agree that their education began (or was resumed) the day they left school.

Where the school system goes wrong is in thinking that education and passing exams are the same thing. They are not. Anything learned in order to pass an exam is immediately forgotten because it is required through compulsion rather than motivation. Certainly I remember the works of Rider Haggard more vividly than those of Virgil. Why weren't we taught something useful, like mending fuses, how plumbing functions, and all the rest of the complex business of how a house works. Or simple book-keeping. Or first aid.

Languages are useful too. I was taught French for about ten years at school, and since then have spent what must add up to about five years in France. I can read French fairly easily but I still feel inhibited about speaking it because always at my back I hear some schoolteacher giving me marks and pulling me up for incorrect use of the conditional or the subjunctive. I was never taught Italian at school, but I did work in Italy and picked up the language as I went along. I now speak it badly, but my Italian accent is better than my French one. School made French an effort. Italian is a pleasure.

And fun and pleasure are what schools ought to be about, and is what they originally were. I've just looked up school in the big Oxford Dictionary and it turns out the word comes from the Greek *skhole* and means leisure spent in the pursuit of knowledge. Schools in recent centuries have been nothing like that. Of course there are teachers who make a subject exciting but they are exceptional. Far more of them turn exciting subjects into mere exam-fodder.

Of course there are some things that school can teach, like conformity and uniformity and discipline and blind obedience and bullying and how to say Sir to some pompous, narrow-minded, sanctimonious, emotional cripple. One good thing about school is that it gives something to react against, and makes the rest of your life a holiday.

36 According to the passage, when children start school they

    A stop learning.

    B become impolite.

    C rarely speak.

    D waste time travelling.

37 The writer remembers Rider Haggard's works because

    A his exam questions were about them.

    B he wanted to read them.

    C he thought he had no ability at languages.

    D the works of Virgil are very boring.

38 The writer of this passage

    A has lived in France for the last five years.

    B still takes French lessons.

    C thinks Italian is easier to learn than French.

    D learnt some Italian without taking any lessons.

39 The writer feels

    A that school made his childhood miserable.

    B angry that other children enjoyed school more than he did.

    C that school should be a place where children learn.

    D that the only positive aspect of school was the holidays.

40 In the first sentence of the last paragraph, the writer's tone is

    A embittered.

    B conciliatory.

    C melancholic.

    D complimentary.

PAPER 2 COMPOSITION 2 hours

*Write **two only** of the following composition exercises. Your answers must follow exactly the instructions given. Write in pen, not pencil. You are allowed to make alterations, but make sure your work is clear and easy to read.*

1   Describe the place where you most like to spend your free time. (About 350 words)

2   What should be done to fight sex discrimination in your country? (About 350 words)

3   Your parents were away on holiday and you were having a party that had got completely out of control. Suddenly you saw them arriving home. Write an account of what followed. (About 350 words)

4   A group of children are going to spend the weekend in the mountains. Write them a note explaining how to use some or all the items below. (About 300 words)

5   Set books

PAPER 3   USE OF ENGLISH   2 hours

SECTION A

1   *Fill each of the numbered blanks in the passage with **one** suitable word.*

Now that America's 'Baby Boomers' – those who started life when the birth-rate was at its peak –
are parents themselves, they are confronted in the child-care sections of the bookshops
with/by (1) material that makes Dr Spock, the gentle guru of their *own* (2) parents'
generation, *seem* (3) very low-tech indeed. It includes flashcards to enable two-year-olds
to learn to read; early education programmes that urge *pregnant* (4) women to talk or sing
didactically to their unborn; experts stressing that it is never too *early* (5) to begin a
musical education and pointing *out* (6) where one can buy a midget violin.

'Superbabies' were a major theme at the latest meeting of The National Association for the
Education of Young Children, but the consensus *was* (7) that force-feeding pre-
schoolers may actually retard *their* (8) intellectual, social and physical development.
Parents *making* (9) Herculean efforts to rear 'superbabies' may instead wind up
with (10) early cases of burn-out on their hands.

Dr George Sterne says that the trend is most noticeable *among* (11) upwardly mobile
young professionals, the excellence-seekers *who* (12) are determined to launch their
offspring on the fast track. '*When (If)* (13) you try too hard to force them to learn things, you
run the *risk* (14) of, first, burn-out, and second, suppressing creativity. Children are
going to learn if they are exposed *to* (15) normal life. They don't need high-tech
curricula to do this.'

What some see *as* (16) the benefits of fast-track learning are *attracting (really)* (17) the
attention of state legislators, _____ (18). In just *about* (19) half the 50 states,
programmes are pending that would *entitle (admit)* (20) children entering school at the age of four.

2   *Finish each of the following sentences in such a way that it is as similar as possible in meaning to the sentence
printed before it.*

Example: I did not find his story convincing.
Answer: I was *not convinced by his story.*

13/20

a   At the end of her speech she thanked the organisers.

She ended *her speech by thanking the organisers.*

b   'There won't be peace until free elections are held', he warned.

He warned that only when *free elections were held would there be
peace*

c She needs your full support if she is to succeed.

7½/14

She needs to be _fully supported by you if she is to succeed._

1

d As you go further, so the risk increases.

The further _you go, the greater the risk_

1

e After the meeting, all the leaders present refused to comment.

2

None _of the leaders present (gave any comment after the_ *accepted to give* _meeting._

f The first chapter was terribly hard to understand.

1

I had _difficulty in understanding the first chapter._ *terrible*

g It would seem that he has been fooled all along.

✗

He would seem _to have been fooled all along_

h They were found in a stolen container left alongside the lorry.

1

They were found in a container _that had stolen and left alongside the lorry._ *been*

3 Fill each of the blanks with a suitable word or phrase.

Example: The police tracked _him down by_ questioning his friends.

✓ a Nowadays I don't have time, but I _used to go_ fishing every weekend when I was younger.

½ b You're overweight, Mr Hill. I'd recommend _you go on_ a diet now. *went*

✓ c I mistook _you for_ someone I knew years ago.

½ d He apologised _for having_ waiting so long. *me* *keeping*

✓ e The jury found him guilty _of attacking_ the bank and the judge passed sentence.

✓ f Having caused two road accidents in a month, he was banned _from driving_ for six months.

5/6

4 For each of the sentences below, write a new sentence as similar as possible in meaning to the original sentence, but using the word given. This word **must not be altered** in any way.

Example: Where should I put all these things?
         go
Answer: *Where do all these things go?*

a She's not playing at her best at the moment.
   form

✓ _She's not in her best form at the moment._

b There are no tickets left for Monday's performance.
   booked

✓ _Monday's performance is fully booked up._

c It's really none of his business.
nothing

✗ ~~He has nothing to do with this~~

d The escaped prisoner has still not been caught.
large

✓ The escaped prisoner is still at large.

e He's been working nonstop since 7 am.
break

✓ He had no break since (he started working at) 7 am

f Do we both have to be there?
compulsory

✗ Is our presence compulsory?

g The subsidy is gradually being withdrawn.
phased

✗ The subsidy is ~~gradually~~ being phased out

h They hadn't been to that part of town before, but he had.
unlike

✓ Unlike him, they hadn't been to that part of town before.

5/10

30/50

SECTION B

5 *Read the following passage, then answer the questions which follow it.*

Airlines are constantly devising new wheezes, presumably to distract the attention of the customers from the fares; if it isn't hot towels, it's propelling pencils, or beds-in-the-baggage-compartment. But British Airways have surely earned this year's IATA Award for Conspicuous Daftness with their latest lark. It is called Fun-Flying (a more implausible conjunction of words can never have been seen since the invention of the Bombay Duck), and it works like this.   5

You pay £35 and go to Heathrow; you have to be there by 10 a.m. You are then directed to a plane, but they don't tell you where it is going. Moreover, you have little hope of finding out even when you get there, because you are not allowed, under the rules, to leave the airport.

But if you don't know where you are going, and indeed can be said only in the most desperately literal sense to have gone there at all, what is the point of the journey? Even with the knowledge   10
that this is the brain-child of an airline, so that nothing is barred for absurdity, few will believe the answer: Fun-Flying enables the Fun-Fliers to buy duty-free goods at the airport to which, blindfolded and gagged, they have been taken.

It is possible, to put it more strongly, that somebody hasn't thought this idea right through. Fun-fliers whose Magical Mystery Tour takes them to Clermont-Ferrand, Stavropol, Trollhättan,   15
Maastricht, Inishmore, Erzurum or Split may find the duty-free facilities there far from lavish; it would be a pity to go all that way (and back) to collect nothing but some tie-dyed skirts and a set of spanners. And even at airports where the display is ample, there must be a limit to the fun that can be extracted from buying a duty-free Walkman, particularly since the same thing is usually available for half the price at your nearest Dixons with the instructions in English.   20

But those who draw the lucky cards, and find themselves in beautiful and romantic spots, are even worse off. Outside, it is Venice or Arles, Granada or a rose-red city half as old as time; but for all the Fun-Flier can see of it, as he listens to the incomprehensible bellowings of the loudspeaker, it might as well be Faskrudsfjordur (regular connections to Breiddalsvik, Hofn and Egilsstadir), and if he sidles nonchalantly towards the exit he will encounter a stewardess with a fiery sword   25
intoning the IATA Oath.

It will never catch on, not just for the reasons given above, but because regular airline passengers will find too little novelty in the scheme. After all, the idea is that you pay through the nose, you are kept in total ignorance, and you are virtually bound to be disappointed. So what else is new?   30

a   What is meant by 'devising new wheezes' (line 1)?

_____

_____

b   What word or phrase could be used in place of 'Daftness' (line 4)?

_____

_____

c   Why is 'Fun-Flying' described as an 'implausible conjunction of words' (line 4)?

_____

_____

d   Why do Fun-Fliers go to their destination 'only in the most desperately literal sense' (lines 9–10)?

_____

_____

e   What reason is given for the statement 'nothing is barred for absurdity' (line 11)?

_____

_____

f   Why are Fun-Fliers described as being 'blindfolded and gagged' (line 13)?

_____

_____

g   Explain the phrase 'somebody hasn't thought this idea right through' (line 14)?

_____

_____

h   Give another expression for 'far from lavish' (line 16).

_____

_____

i   Explain what the writer means when he says 'there must be a limit to the fun that can be extracted from buying a duty-free Walkman' (lines 18–19).

_____

_____

j   Why are Fun-Fliers who go to attractive places 'even worse off' (line 22)?

_____

_____

k What does 'it' on line 27 refer to?

_____

_____

l What is meant by 'catch on' (line 27)?

_____

_____

m What are 'regular airline passengers' (line 27)?

_____

_____

n What is implied about the service they usually get?

_____

_____

_____

_____

o In a paragraph of 60–80 words, explain what Fun-Flying is and what the drawbacks are.

_____

_____

_____

_____

_____

_____

_____

_____

_____

_____

_____

PAPER 4   LISTENING COMPREHENSION   about 30 minutes

FIRST PART

For question 1 tick one of the boxes A, B, C or D next to the correct picture.

1   What does the foldaway tool kit consist of?

A · B · C · D

A		B		C		D	

For questions 2–4 tick one of the boxes A, B, C or D

2   Which is the cheapest?

   A   the key ring

   B   the bed

   C   the radio

   D   the pen

A	
B	
C	
D	

3   Which is the lightest in weight?

   A   the radio

   B   the jewellery case

   C   the bed

   D   the fishing rod

A	
B	
C	
D	

4   Which is sold with the most items inside?

   A   the fishing rod bag

   B   the tool kit

   C   the jewellery case

   D   the first aid kit

A	
B	
C	
D	

SECOND PART

*For questions **5–9** put a tick in **one** of the boxes **A**, **B**, **C** or **D**.*

5   According to the speaker, how many door-to-door salesmen can you trust?

    A   All of them.

    B   Most of them.

    C   Few of them.

    D   None of them.

A	
B	
C	
D	

6   An unscrupulous salesman might

    A   damage or break into your home.

    B   claim that you cannot afford the product.

    C   offer to buy your house.

    D   pretend to make you a special offer.

A	
B	
C	
D	

7   The 'hard-luck story' aims to make you feel

    A   sorry for the salesman.

    B   envious of your neighbours.

    C   less fortunate than your friends.

    D   delighted with the product.

A	
B	
C	
D	

8   Which of the following should you never do at home?

    A   Buy anything from door-to-door salesmen.

    B   Buy without comparing prices.

    C   Buy on hire purchase.

    D   Buy encyclopaedias.

A	
B	
C	
D	

9   Members of the Direct Selling Association

    A   never employ door-to-door salesmen.

    B   guarantee some of their products.

    C   will wait a fortnight for payment.

    D   offer a two-week cooling-off period.

A	
B	
C	
D	

THIRD PART

10 *For question **10** tick whether you think the statements are **true** or **false**.*

	True	False

a Jackson used to be a musician.

b He has already been to Milan.

c In the UK it is illegal to spray graffiti in public places.

d Jackson meets many other graffiti artists on the street.

e He taught Plant how to use a spray can.

f Plant told the prosecutor that he regretted his action.

g He sometimes decorates people's homes with graffiti.

h He says that graffiti is an integral part of street culture.

i Where he lives, people only care about their own specialities.

j The local police have given up trying to catch graff-ites.

FOURTH PART

11 *For question **11**, tick the boxes to show which suggestions are made.*

a Lose his car and flat keys.

b Throw food on his carpet.

c Have a chat with his wife.

d Run up a huge telephone bill.

e Put dog food in his meals.

f Break eggs under his carpet.

g Set fire to all his shoes.

h Ruin his best towels.

i Erase his sports videos.

j Burn his favourite novels.

*For question **12** tick **one** of the boxes **A**, **B**, **C** or **D**.*

12 'Naturally, we wouldn't want you to try these, girls.' The tone of this remark

A advises listeners against trying these ideas.

B suggests these ideas are impracticable.

C encourages listeners to try these ideas.

D implies that other ideas are better.

A	
B	
C	
D	

PAPER 5 INTERVIEW

The theme of this Test is **Plants**.

1 a Look at *one* of the photographs and describe:
  ☐ the scene
  ☐ the people
  ☐ what they are doing, and why

  If you are doing the interview in a group, compare the scene and the people in your picture with those in the others'.

  b Now discuss:
  ☐ the ecological damage caused by farming
  ☐ the appeal of flowers and house plants
  ☐ agriculture in your country

2   Study *one* of these passages. You may quote from it if you wish.

a   It looks rather like oversized rhubarb, grows several metres a year and can force its way up through road surfaces, eventually taking over whole areas in country and town alike. Knotweed's roots can survive cutting, burning or even herbicides that wipe out everything else in sight; while importing the insects which control it in its native Japan would put other flora and fauna at risk.

b   Why are raw carrots so tasty! What makes a blade of grass so nice to nibble on a hot summer's day? Why does bread taste sweet if you chew it long enough? The answer of course is the presence of sugars. And the extract from beet and cane is versatile: bottles and windows that shatter in the movies are made of it, flowers in a vase stay fresh longer with a spoonful in the water, and when your mouth's on fire after a curry – try a lump or two.

c   The flock of birds on your lawn, the ladybirds, beetles and innumerable wildlife in the garden are all busy accounting for many millions of pests daily. WE CANNOT DO WITHOUT THEM, so don't kill them with chemicals.

   Make room somewhere in the garden for a few weeds – which are only wild flowers. These will provide a habitat for insects, which form an important part of many predators' diets.

   Organic gardening depends on the whole intricate web of wildlife to ensure that there is always a balance of pests and predators.

Where do you think the text is taken from?
Who do you think the speaker or writer might be?
What is the purpose of the text?
Discuss the content.

3   Do *one* of these tasks.

a   Imagine the council in your town has plans to turn your favourite woodland area into a shopping centre: you are part of an Action Committee set up to fight them. Put forward your views, considering the guidelines given below:
   ☐   the destruction of an area of outstanding natural beauty
   ☐   the damage to local plant and animal life
   ☐   the loss of one of the community's best leisure areas
   ☐   the questionable need for yet more shopping facilities
   ☐   alternative sites for the buildings

b   Look at the advertisement below and then discuss the following:

THEY DIE, YOU DIE

Imagine your fate is entwined with that of a South American vine, or a fragile pink flower in far off Madagascar.

If these plants were threatened with extinction, you would spring to their defence.

What if we told you that many patients facing major surgery rely on a muscle relaxant extracted from an Amazonian vine, Chondrodendron tomentosum? Or that 4 out of 5 children with leukaemia survive, thanks to the chemicals vineristine and vinblastine donated by the rosy periwinkle?

Would the fate of these plants still arouse your concern? If so, read on. It is essential that you be aroused beyond mere concern, to action.

Millions of people with heart ailments depend on foxgloves. These flowers provide the digoxin which regulates their heartbeat.

Extracts from an Amazonian oak tree coagulate proteins, immensely helping scientists in their search for an AIDS vaccine.

Though these plants have healed and soothed millions of people, they're but the merest sample from nature's medicine chest. Over a quarter of all prescribed medicines are based on plants. Now this vast store of known and potential medicines is under threat and we are all of us obliged to protect it. You see, half of the earth's species thrive in the warmth and wetness of tropical rainforests. Just ten square kilometres of Amazonian jungle contain some 2,200 species of plant.

Man is destroying these rainforests. 40 hectares a minute. An area the size of Austria every year. Every day, 5 plants silently become extinct.

Join WWF — World Wildlife Fund For

Nature, and help reverse this process of destruction. For almost 30 years WWF has lobbied governments and institutions, battling and educating in the name of conservation. Our latest battle plan covers 132 projects aimed at saving the earth's biological diversity, the intricate inter-dependence of ecosystems of which plants are the basis. We need a further US $60 million to fund these projects through the next 5 years.

Join our fight. Help save the plants and organisms which ease the pain and save the lives of humans. Help with your money, your work, your voice. Start by writing to the WWF National Organisation in your country or the Membership Secretary, WWF International, CH — 1196 Gland, Switzerland, right now. It's do or die.

   ☐   the importance of plants to medicine
   ☐   how plant life can be protected
   ☐   what you could do to help

PAPER 3 SECTION B SAMPLES

SAMPLE 1

SECTION B

5 *Read the following passage, then answer the questions which follow it.*

WHEN A PHONE-IN SOUNDS LIKE FAWNING

Phone-ins are everywhere, on the BBC, commercial radio and the World Service. They are cheap, satisfy a craving for instant fame and exude a strong whiff of democracy. Yet there are lingering doubts about their value.

First of all, imposters can get through. A famous example occurred last year, when hundreds of thousands of listeners heard an angry man from Doncaster ring up to savage Michael Green, 5 controller of Radio 4, for the appalling soap opera Citizens. It was an electrifying moment, and Green sounded rattled by the ferocity of the criticism. Later it emerged that the caller was in fact the former producer of Start the Week and a lover of cruel practical jokes. He had given a false name when he rang.

This year there have been other worries. Does the BBC give its controllers an easy ride? Are 10 these programmes PR masquerading as journalism? During the phone-in with Radio 4's controller earlier this month, I observed the proceedings from start to finish. Once, I naïvely imagined that when you listened to a BBC phone-in what you heard was simply a succession of people ringing the BBC. If they got through, they were put on the air and asked their questions. The very opposite is true: they are on the air because the BBC has called *them*. 15

Lines open at 8am. There is one number to ring, and eight lines on it. Each of the eight extension phones in the Broadcasting House basement is manned by a BBC production assistant or secretary – volunteers working overtime. If you get through, you speak to one them for several minutes. They have printed forms on which they write your name, phone number, age bracket, gender, a summary of your question and a category called 'on air potential – good/average/poor'. 20 The volunteers have to put a tick against one of them. 'Those marked 'poor' aren't chosen,' said Caroline Millington, head of BBC radio's magazine programmes. 'They would probably freeze on air.'

The forms are handed to the deputy producer, Chris Paling. Promising questions he puts in a separate pile, summarising the question at the top of the sheet and running a yellow highlight pen 25 through it. He hands this pile to Nick Utechin, the producer, who makes the final selection and also decides the running order of the calls, in order to get a varied menu. A woman telephonist rings back the chosen callers and keeps them on the telephone until their big moment, when they are put on the air. Presenter Nick Ross knows the name and town of each caller, and who is coming up next, because that information is flashed on to a television monitor which he and 30 Utechin can see but Green cannot.

On the basis of what I saw, Paling and Utechin selected exactly those questions which any other seasoned journalists would have done to create the most lively programme possible. I saw several questions from admiring callers who 'liked Radio 4 a lot': none of them made it past Paling's desk.

You have to be very persistent. The BBC estimates that about 3,000 callers tried to ring the 35 Radio 4 phone-in. Of those, 204 got through and logged their questions; 16 were chosen to go on the air. On Radio 3's phone-in, 185 callers got through and once again 16 were chosen. So even if you do succeed in getting through, the chances of then getting on the air are still more than 10–1 against.

Even though the programmes try not to be bland, they have one great defect. The controllers 40 are interviewed by their own employees as well as by their listeners: Green by Ross, for example. Isn't it a bit much to expect someone to interrogate freely and without fear or favour the very person who pays their salary? At the moment, presenters have vested financial interests in not being too rude or too curious. A little network-swapping would be no bad thing, and would give the BBC's controllers a more testing time. 45

a Why, according to the text, are there so many radio phone-in programmes?

_____

b Who or what are 'imposters' (line 4) in this context?

_____

c What is 'Start the Week' and why is it mentioned?

_____

d How does the author answer the question 'Does the BBC give its controllers an easy ride?' (line 10)?

_____

e Explain the meaning of 'PR masquerading as journalism' (line 11).

_____

f Why does the author use the word 'naïvely' (line 12)?

_____

g What does 'them' on line 21 refer to?

_____

h What is meant by 'freeze' as it is used on line 22?

_____

i Explain the phrase 'Promising questions' as it is used in the text. (line 24).

_____

j What have the callers been doing just before they go on the air?

_____

k What is it that Green is not shown?

_____

l What happened to the 'questions' referred to on line 34, and what was the reason for this?

_____

m What does '10–1 against' (line 38) mean in this context?

_____

n What suggestion does the author make in the last sentence, and why?

_____

o   In a paragraph of 60–80 words, summarise the steps that listeners must take to participate in BBC phone-ins, and state the factors that determine which people are selected to do so.

_____

_____

_____

_____

_____

_____

_____

_____

_____

_____

SAMPLE 1 CANDIDATE ANSWERS

CINTA

a Because they are cheap, and they satisfy a large crowd. (1)

b They are the ones who give a false name so as not to reveal their own identification. (½)

c 'Start the Week' is a soap opera and it is mentioned because the man who criticized the soap opera 'Citizens' happened to be the former producer of 'Start the Week'? (1)

d They give its controllers an easy ride because the calls that are put on the air are chosen by the BBC, so they avoid conflictive calls, and the controllers are more or less prepared because they know the main subject of what they are going to be asked. (1)

e Are these programmes PR considered as journalism? (0)

f He uses the adverb naïvely to show us that he imagined it in an innocent way, and that he couldn't imagine that the very opposite could take place. (1)

g 'them' is referred to one of those categories called on air potentia, that is, good, average or poor. (1)

h It is meant that they would probably be considered boring questions without any interest at all. (0)

i It means that those questions which have some interest and have a high probability to be put on the air are separated from those which have no interest. (1)

j The chosen callers have been phoned back and they have been kept on the phone until they go on the air. (1)

k The name and town of each caller and the order of the callers aren't shown to Green because he is the controller and this information is only shown to the presenter and the producer as it is flashed on to a television monitor. (1)

l Those questions weren't chosen by Paling because they didn't want admiring callers specially those ones who loved Radio 4. (1½)

m That your chances of getting on the air are very few, you may have one chance out of 10 possibilities. (1)

n He suggests to do a network-swapping, that is, a change in the working structure and in the interviewers in order to interrogate freely and without any fear. (½)

o You have to dial the number and be very persistent if you want to get through. Then you speak to a secretary who writes down the main details and the grade of interest of the questions. These forms are handed to the deputy producer who selects the best ones and gives them to the producer who makes the final selection and decides the order of the calls. Then a telephonist rings back the chosen callers and keeps them on the telephone until they are put on the air. (5)

Total: 16½/32

Examiner's comments

This candidate obviously has a clear understanding of the text, and has included the relevant information in the majority of the answers. However marks have been lost as a result of the candidate failing to explain why the information is relevant, eg **l** why did they not want admiring calls?, similarly in **n** network-swapping is mentioned but the reasons for it are not made clear.

The summary gives the basic steps a listener must take to participate, but ignores the second part of the question, ie the factors that determine the selection of people. Instead irrelevant details about the selection of questions is included, irrelevant information is also included in **k**, the question does not ask 'why?' only 'what?'.

MARIA

a Because they are cheap, make people famous for an instant and that satisfies them and it has a lot of democracy. (2)

b Imposters are those ones who get through by not telling the truth. In the programme they talk about an absolutely different thing from the one they've told the volunteers. For doing this they give a false name. (½)

c Start the Week is another programme of phone-ins and they mention it because the imposter worked in that programme. (and he wanted that Michael Green lose fame). The imposter was the former producer of Start the Week. (½)

d Controllers are given an easy ride. The author make us know it by telling us the way callers are chosen. (½)

e   not showing the truth clearly, disguising the truth as journalists do as a way or
    propaganda. (0)
f   Inocently, as child believes everything. Because he wants to make us realise that he
    believed it inocently, as childs. They believe everything. ($\frac{1}{2}$)
g   Them refers to the different categories. ($\frac{1}{2}$)
h   Not going very far, you make the question and as it is not interesting it will be kept on
    the air, nobody will be interested in it. (0)
i   He separate the questions that seem to be very interesting. Those ones that he thinks
    are going to have a lot to discuss or to say about them, he separates them from the
    others. He marks them with a yellow highlight pen. (1)
j   Just before, they have been waiting on the phone for their big moment. The
    telephonist have rung them and made them keep on the phone until their moment
    arrives. (1)
k   Green can't see a television monitor in which appears the name and the town of each
    caller because he doesn't have to know who is going to interview him and what the
    question is going to be like. (1)
l   They reached Paling's desk but they didn't go further because what Paling and
    Uteching wanted was to make a live programme, different from the others, and those
    questions are the ones every journalist chooses. They are not interesting questions. (1)
m   That you have one possibility of getting trough against ten possibilities of not getting
    through. or more (1)
n   Controllers should work independently, and test would be more interesting (0)
o   First of all they have to phone the BBC and talk with a production assistant for
    several minutes. He will fill in a printed form where he will write their personal
    details and he will give a mark to their questions (poor, average . . .). The forms that
    contain interesting questions are handed to the deputy producer, who will separate
    the ones that seem more interesting to hand them to Nick Utechin, who is the one
    that will make the final selection. When the running order is decided, a telephonist
    rings back the chosen person and they are kept on the phone until the moment
    arrives. People selected are those ones who seem to be interesting, and those ones
    who are persistent because is really difficult getting through. (6)

Total=15$\frac{1}{2}$/32

Examiners' comments

The language level of this answer is fair, although the candidate has lost marks for including
subjective comment and details which are not included in the text eg **b** we are not told that
imposters change the subject when they are on the air, and in **f** the candidate stresses the
innocence of children, which is not relevant to the answer. In addition irrelevant material has also
been lifted from the text eg in **i** we are not asked what happens to the 'promising questions' only
what they are, and in the summary the question selection procedure is not required.

As a whole the summary is fair, the main points are included, although the candidate would be
penalised for the inclusion of irrelevant material.

MARIEL

a   One of the reasons is because they are cheap. Another reason is because people like
    to call and be on air, thinking that they are famous for a while; and the third reason
    the text says is because these programmes are democratic, and everybody can ask and
    say what they want to know, freely; I mean the programmes seem to be a way for
    people to express their ideas, at least, they seem to be so, though they really aren't. (3)
b   People who call this programmes with the aim of disturbing; they are going to say
    thing which aren't good, they are going to try to embarras the controller; they are
    like maniacs in a way. (0)
c   Start the week is another radio programme. (1)
d   Initially, he answers with another question, but on the text we can find another
    answer; yes, the BBC gives them an easy ride, preparing the programmes a lot. ($\frac{1}{2}$)
e   Ways of hiding real experienced questions that a journalist would prepare to make a
    good programme. (0)

f   To say that he is not sure of what happens really. He imagined that it occured that way, but without anything that made him think that way. I mean, without having seen anything, or heard anything, only with the things in his mind. He imagined it in an innocent way. $(\frac{1}{2})$

g   The people who are going to make questions on the air, the ones who are chosen by the radio producers to make the question.   (0)

h   They would probably get so embarrassed on air, that they wouldn't say a word, and wouldn't make the question.   (1)

i   The questions that could be interesting to make in the programme, the ones which are selected in this first selection, are put together, separate from the non-interesting ones, in a pile. This selected ones will be given to the producer.   (1)

j   They have been waiting on the telephone. They have to wait for their moment to make the question. A telephonist had rang them and they have to wait on the phone.   (1)

k   The name and town of each caller, and who is coming up next.   (1)

l   These question wouldn't past Paling's desk, I mean, are not selected. They don't want these questions because they aren't interesting for the listeners, and they want to look like a serious programme which accepts questions from 'the enemy', I mean, from people who really want to make difficult and interesting questions, not only from admiring callers.   (2)

m You have less than 1 possibility of getting on the air, against 10 possibilities of not getting.   (1)

n   That the controllers should not be interviewed by their employees because the employees cannot choose freely the most interesting questions, since they are questioning their employers. The suggestion is because now, the programme is a fictitious one. The questions are not democratic and don't show what people really want to know.   (0)

o   The steps that listeners must take to participate in BBC phone-ins are the following ones: they have to ring the number of the Broadcasting House and speak to one of the production assistant or secretary. The ringers give their name, phone number, etc and say their questions. The telephone call finishes; and then, if their questions are selected, a telephonist will ring them back to make their questions on the air. The factors that determine which people are selected to do so are: the kind of question they make and the way the would speak on the air; I mean, if they are very nervous, or embarrassed, or something like that.   (9)

Total=21/30

Examiners' comments

The level of language in this answer is good, and the writing is coherent and in most cases relevant, although in **l** and the summary the repetition of 'I mean' is more appropriate to the spoken rather than the written form. Marks have been lost where the candidate failed to answer all parts of the question, eg **c** and **n**, in the latter irrelevant material from the last paragraph of the text is followed by a very vague reference to the suggestion about which the question asks. In **f** and **l** the tense of the question has not been noted when writing the answer, although the information contained in the answers is largely correct, the candidate could be penalised. The summary paragraph is well composed, and both parts of the question have been dealt with, although the last sentence tends to trail off.

SAMPLE 2

SECTION B

5 *Read the following passage, then answer the questions which follow it.*

HAVE WE REACHED OUR PEAK BEFORE THIRTYSOMETHING?

Studies have repeatedly shown that in a wide variety of fields, people are at their most productive and creative in early adulthood and then undergo a steady decline. But while psychologists have studied this curious decline in achievement from virtually every perspective – finding it among both geniuses and laggards, among everyone from composers to chemists – they have no real understanding of why it happens. 5

Researchers do know that the age at which this peak occurs differs according to profession. People who rely on pure bursts of creativity – for example physicists, theoretical mathematicians and poets – tend to produce their most original work in their late twenties and early thirties. The output of novelists, engineers and medical researchers, on the other hand, tends to rise more slowly, peaking in the late thirties and early forties, and then falling steadily until retirement. 10

But is this curious achievement cycle an inevitable function of ageing? Or is it the result of some other phenomenon that, if understood more completely, could be managed to prolong creativity?

It is difficult to account for the effect of age because the most obvious explanations – that as people age, their physical health and mental capacity may deteriorate – do not hold up to close scrutiny. A mathematician whose best days are behind him at 35, for example, clearly is not any 15 less intelligent than at 25. Another common idea is that as people enter middle age, they become either distracted by new responsibilities or lulled into complacency by academic tenure or job promotions. But the social demands of early adulthood – courtship, establishing a family, financial difficulty – are potentially as much an impediment to productivity as professional gatekeeper responsibilities. 20

More than 100 years ago, psychologist GM Beard pioneered a different approach, arguing that productivity was the combination of enthusiasm and experience. Enthusiasm, he said, is abundant in the beginning of professional life, then declines gradually. Experience, by contrast, starts from zero and grows over the course of a career. According to Beard, enthusiasm without experience renders original but unfocused effort, while experience without enthusiasm results in uninspired 25 work. But during those years when the two curves intersect, Beard maintained, productive creativity would be at its peak. The strength of this theory is that it explains why peaks differ from field to field. Poetry, some say, requires more creativity than experience, so poets do their best work in their twenties. But historians, for example, might need a vast amount of experience and just a touch of enthusiasm, so their work might not begin to shine until much later. 30

But Beard's ideas are too simplistic for modern psychologists. For one thing, his theory implies that at either end of a career peak, work would suffer not just in quantity but also in quality, since most output would be ruined by either too little experience or too little enthusiasm. But do people really go into these kinds of pre- and post-peak slumps? A number of contemporary researchers say that, in fact, the ratio of high-quality work to poor-quality work never changes during a typical 35 career. In other words, a genius biologist who wins awards for 70 percent of his papers at age 25 will still have the same high percentage of brilliant papers at age 60. The difference is that in youth he might write 10 papers a year but later in life drop to two a year.

University of California psychologist Dean Keith Simonton argues for a more complex explanation. Like Beard, he assumes that ideas come tumbling out at the beginning of a career. He 40 says, however, that peak creativity comes not with experience but when individuals complete the secondary step of giving those ideas shape. Simonton's explanations for why different careers peak at different times is that some ideas take longer to develop than others. A poet may need just five years, an epidemiologist 25. Simonton says his theory leads to two happy conclusions. The first is that getting and developing ideas is not a biological function of age but rather the typical 45 consequence of being faced with a new intellectual environment. As a result, an ageing society need not be unproductive if people enter new fields after their productivity peaks in a previous field. The other conclusion is that when you peak depends on how many ideas you have.

a In your own words, explain what happens to people's work as they get older.

_____

b What have studies failed to show?

_____

c In what way do 'physicists, theoretical mathematicians and poets' (line 7) tend to create their work?

_____

d What often happens to novelists' work when they are about 40?

_____

e Explain 'managed' as it is used on line 12.

_____

f What is the writer's opinion of the 'explanations' on line 13?

_____

g Explain the factors that may reduce young people's productivity.

_____

_____

h When, according to Beard, does experience develop? How does its absence harm people's work?

_____

_____

i What fact supports Beard's theory?

_____

j What are 'post-peak slumps' (line 34)?

_____

k What effect does age have on the work done by a 'genius biologist' (line 36)?

_____

l What do Beard's and Simonton's theories have in common? How do they differ?

_____

_____

m What, according to Simonton, should people do when they have passed the most successful part of their careers?

_____

n In a paragraph of 70–90 words, state all the reasons that have been suggested to explain why professional achievement declines with age.

_____

_____

_____

_____

_____

_____

_____

_____

_____

_____

SAMPLE 2 CANDIDATE ANSWERS

DAISUKE

a people's work generally tends to be less productive and less creative as they get older after passing their peaks. (1)

b The studies failed to show why the decline in achievement happens when people get older. (1)

c They tend to create their work by creativity oriented (0)

d Their work goes to a peak and falls steadily until retirement. (1)

e to control their creativity as long as they could (0)

f He thinks that explanations have not yet been well done. (0)

g The social demand and proffesional gate keeper responsibilities distract their productivity. ($\frac{1}{2}$)

h Experience develops over the course of a career, It's absence harms people's work because it tends to be diviated to the wrong directions. (1)

i Each field of careers have different peaks of achivement. ($\frac{1}{2}$)

j Their work suffers in quantity but also in quality (0)

k The work has not been changed in quality but declined in productivity. ($\frac{1}{2}$)

l People need to have enough experience to come to peak creativity Simonton points out that age is not the factor but facing with a new environment is indispensable. (0)

m People should try to challenge new fields after passing productivity peaks in a previous career. (1)

n A biological functions such as their health and mental capacity may deteriorate. As people enter middle age they tend to be distracted by their life including but not limited to responsibilities and social status and demands. As people get older, their enthusiasm diclines gradually and results in uninspired work. People have little chance to face with a new intelligent environment and get less new ideas in their mind. (4)

Total=10$\frac{1}{2}$/30

Examiners' comments

The language level in this answer is good but the candidate loses of lot of marks through failing to answer a lot of the questions accurately or precisely enough, eg **c** is not a complete answer, a noun is needed to complete the sentence, and in **f** the misuse of 'well done' means that the answer is incorrect, though the idea is probably correct. Inattention to grammatical form also loses the candidate marks, eg in **i** the answer is correct but very badly written, with simple spelling mistakes as well as basic grammatical errors. The summary is too brief, several of the relevant points are listed, but the candidate has made no effort to join them together into a cohesive paragraph: as marks are awarded for the structure of the paragraph as well as the factual content it is very important that candidates think carefully about the cohesion of the summary.

RITA

a People's creativity and productivity at an older age is lagging behind the output at earlier ages. ($\frac{1}{2}$)

b The studies couldn't find the reasons for this phenomenon. (1)

c Their success depends mostly on personal abilities, so they can achieve the peak at an early age. (0)

d Novelists are often sentenced to decline in the second half of their lifes. ($\frac{1}{2}$)

e Managed means used in that sentence. (1)

f In his opinion the reasons given by psychologist are not enough accurate and exact. $(\frac{1}{2})$

g The lack of experience and the responsibilities of staring an independent life after school can build disadvantages for young people. $(\frac{1}{2})$

h According to Beard experience grows with age and its lack can affect badly the value of a completed work. $(\frac{1}{2})$

i His theory is able to give an acceptable explanation for the differences in peaks. $(\frac{1}{2})$

j These are periods after middle age, when people can't provide the highest efficiency any more. (1)

k His output declines in number but not in quality. $(\frac{1}{2})$

l They both agree that young people are full of new ideas, but Simonton says , that the peak is achieved with the realisation of an idea, not with experience. (2)

m They should try to search for new jobs, problems, ideas – change makes life interesting. (1)

n One of the explanations is that people's body and mind undergoes a decline with age. Another possibility is that the concentration on work is affected by other responsibilities coming with age. The decline in enthusiasm after middle age is as well a reasonable argument. We shouldn't forget the reduction in the number of ideas. The last given reason is that people usually do not face new fields after they completed or realized one job or idea. (8)

Total $= 17\frac{1}{2}/30$

Examiners' comments

The language level in this answer is very good, but the candidate loses a lot of marks through failing to answer the question completely, eg in **i** the candidate mentions the differences in peaks, but fails to say that these peaks are of different professions, also in **l** what the theories have in common is given, but how they differ is not clear as only Simonton's view is given in the second part of the answer. Subjective interpretation is another factor which loses the candidate marks e.g. in **d** the candidate says that novelists are often 'sentenced' to decline, which could suggest an external influence. A straightforward statement of fact is what the question requires. Similarly in **g** the candidate summarises the factors that may reduce the productivity of young people in the phrase 'the responsibilities of starting an independent life after school', this is a subjective interpretation, the answers are in fact in the text and should be extracted, not interpreted.

The summary is well written, most of the reasons have been given, and the paragraph is cohesive and well developed, the candidate having made good use of linking devices.

SANDRA

a Their productivity and creativity steadily declines. (1)

b The reason for the decline in achievement (1)

c In bliss meaning a short period of time, in which they are very creative. $(\frac{1}{2})$

d This is the time their creativity reaches its highest point (1)

e The phenomenon could be used to make creativity last longer. (1)

f He doesn't believe them, they can be proven unlikely very easily. $(1\frac{1}{2})$

g They have other problems to think about for example establishing a family, which is a new experience often they also have financial problems following this. (2)

h It grows during a career, without experience the work is unfocused, meaning that it's unclear not as professional as with experience. (2)

i That the peaks differ from profession to profession (1)

j The curve of productivity decreasing after a peak (1)

k He writes less than in his youth, but the quality of his work stays the same. (1)

l   In common: creativity is very high at the beginning of a career. Differ: peaks don't come with experience but when the ideas are given shape.   (2)

m   They should enter a new field, start with something different.   (1)

n   The first explanation is that health and mental capacity deteriorate as people get older. As another reason they say that the responsibilities for people in their middle age become bigger for instance with a new job. People might also get academical jobs and so become fixed of developing new ideas maybe also out of lack of time. Another reason they give is that productivity declines when a person has run out of ideas what tends to happen as you get older.   (8)

Total = 24/30

Examiners' comments

This answer is very well written, the candidate has answered all of the questions, most of the answers being concise and accurate. The language level is very good, the answers each closely correspond to the format of the question, thus it is clear that the candidate has read the questions carefully and considered the subject and the tense in each answer. Some marks have been lost through a failure to answer all parts of the question, eg in **g** not all the factors given in the text have been included, and in **l** how the theories differ has not been fully explained.

The summary is very good, the paragraph is well developed, with the inclusion of most of the reasons for the decline of professional achievement with age.

LISTENING SCRIPTS

TEST ONE: First Part

You will hear an extract from a radio programme about the effects of noise on people. For questions 1–4 tick one of the boxes A, B, C or D. You will hear the piece twice.

Int: . . . . . . and now onto a subject that's been getting an increasing amount of attention recently: noise. Mike Day of Salford University is currently doing research into its effects on health. Mike:

Day: Well, one thing we know for sure is that different noises have different effects on people. A lot of work's already been done on the kinds of noise one associates with industry – things like heavy vehicles, ventilation systems, pneumatic drills and so on, or the noise generated by electrical appliances – so we've been studying the sound of people talking in places such as open-plan offices where voices are often overheard. What we've discovered is that this kind of noise affects people at much lower levels than was previously thought.

Now, while industrial noise below about 60 decibels apparently has little effect, irrelevant speech can be a real problem at considerably lower levels than this. And what this means is that we need a reduction of more than 20 decibels if office workers are not to be affected: much more difficult to achieve than the relatively small drop in sound level required to eliminate the effects of mechanical or electrical noise.

Int: How in practice are people affected by this noise?

Day: Well, in a way that might encourage employers to actually do something about the problem: the stress it causes makes staff work less efficiently, particularly when they have to use their memory for things like remembering numbers and other details – from phone messages for instance. Now this can happen even when the noise level is not all that high, which is interesting because some tasks can be performed perfectly well even at levels where the person's hearing could be damaged.

Int: But most can't, surely?

Day: Oh no, of course not. For example, researchers in California have been looking at how aeroplane take-off noise affects the behaviour of children living in the vicinity. Their study shows quite conclusively that the noise not only brings about physiological changes but also has an adverse effect on their school work.

Int: So what's your next project?

Day: I think we ought now to be getting into the workplace rather than spending more time doing research in laboratory conditions, so we're going to have a close look at how noise affects people at work in terms of their health, how well they perform, and how they actually feel . . . . whether they feel tense, or disorientated, or whatever.

Int: Thanks, Mike.

Now listen to the piece again.

TEST ONE: Second Part

You will hear an extract from a lecture on phobias. For question 5 fill in the blanks in the diagrams. You will hear the piece twice.

For the estimated one in 12 people who suffer from a phobia, life can be governed by their irrational fear. Everyday situations become the source of acute anxiety, and life a battle.

Problems include agoraphobia, fear of animals or objects, fear of sex, and compulsive/obsessive behaviour such as the Lady Macbeth syndrome – an obsessive fear of being dirty which leads people compulsively to wash hundreds of times a day. Some wash all the time for fear of passing germs on to their children.

One woman stole soap and disinfectant from shops, so expensive was her compulsion to maintain. When she was finally caught, the police were unable to take her fingerprints because the skin on her fingertips was rubbed smooth. Conversely, the painter Chaïm Soutine was afraid to wash for fear of losing his artistic talent.

Some people have been known to adopt a liquids-only diet because swallowing food has become so fearsome. Claustrophobia led an unfortunate roofing specialist to climb the stairs of London's Post Office Tower twice a day because he could not use the lift. And a woman afraid of false hair made special appointments with her hairdresser so he could hide all the wigs in the shop.

Cases are documented of people being terrified by telephones, knives, and by having to write in public. People have been treated for fear of cigarette smoke, of tunnels or bridges, of hearing running water, of blushing, of white shirts, even of reading. Now fear of Aids has become the most modern phobia recorded.

The most common is the fear of going outside or into crowds. It is estimated that there may be two million sufferers in the UK, and while other phobias tend to affect both sexes equally, two thirds of agoraphobics are women.

In severe cases, the problem prevents people from leaving their homes, but many sufferers manage to hold down a job, concealing their fear of specific situations. They may be terrified of travelling on trains – while being reasonably happy to drive a car. Or they may travel to work at 6 am to avoid the rush hour.

Various other tricks have been reported: gripping a case or umbrella while outside, chewing gum to calm the nerves or wearing dark glasses. One agoraphobic felt an urge to strip when struck by panic. She always wore clothes fastened by zips just in case and carried a pair of scissors with her – to reassure herself she could get out of her clothes in no time at all.

Those with severe phobias will go to extreme lengths to avoid contact with whatever terrifies them. One woman jumped out of a moving car when she spotted a spider. Another sufferer from spider phobia reached a point at which she felt suicidal. For her, the first small step to recovery was drawing black circles on paper to represent spiders. Later, she managed to look at pictures of them.

For those who have never suffered from a phobia, the idea that someone could be suicidal over spiders seems bizarre. Many people have a cautious dislike of spiders, but show little sympathy to those for whom the sight of the creatures induces terror.

But even those whose phobias are very deep-rooted can still treat themselves . . .

Now listen to the piece again.

TEST ONE: Third Part

You will hear a report on travel sickness. For questions 6–11 tick one of the boxes A, B, C, or D. You will hear the piece twice.

Pat: Motion sickness may take the form of nausea, giddiness, fatigue and even depression. Maggie Davies has been taking a look at some of the remedies.

Maggie: Here's a recipe for disaster: strap a small child into the back of a car, light up a cigarette, turn on the stereo and set off on a fun drive. Make sure to brake whenever possible, roar up hill and down dale pointing out the cows on the left, the piggies on the right and the hedgehog running for its life across the road. You will probably have a case of travel sickness on your hands.

Motion sickness is no respecter of persons: in a heavy gale, even the most hardened sailor may succumb. A relatively stable journey also will induce nausea if the air in a car or cabin is stuffy. Other factors – fumes, for example, or the sight of food – can make the condition worse. For chronic sufferers, anxiety based on previous attacks can be a contributory factor.

Motion sickness is caused by a mismatch of sensory information reaching the brain. Unusual, repetitive movement confuses the senses and disturbs the delicate machanisms controlling balance in the inner ear. The result is giddiness, sweating, headache, vomiting and sometimes fatigue, apathy and depression. Experience of nausea creates a dread of sickness; dread, in turn, triggers nausea.

David Williams, a general practitioner from Surrey and an amateur sailor who has provided medical cover on the *Lord Nelson*, a tall ship equipped for a disabled crew, uses a mixture of orthodox and 'alternative' treatments. Depending on the individual, he might prescribe anti-histamine drugs such as hyoscine to help prevent motion sickness or a homeopathic compound. Homeopathy works on the principle of similarity, so nausea might be treated with dilute preparations of nauseants such as borax, petroleum or tabacum.

Ginger has been used by the Chinese as an anti-nauseant for 2,000 years. Dr Williams himself chews crystallised ginger and recommends ginger biscuits for car-sick children. He also uses acupuncture for sea-sickness – 'to miraculous effect', according to one prostrate sailor on the *Lord Nelson*.

Many travellers and chemists recommend Sea Bands, elasticated bracelets with a plastic button placed over the acupressure point on both wrists. However, there is no scientific evidence that they work: controlled trials carried out by the Royal Navy were inconclusive.

About 60 per cent of RAF cadets suffer motion sickness. Recruits undergo a month-long programme of de-sensitisation that takes them from simulated flights and gentle airborne manoeuvres to more vigorous aerobatics. The treatment, carried out by Alan Benson, senior medical officer at the RAF's Institute of Aviation Medicine in Farnborough, is successful for almost all of the RAF's intake. Those who remain prone to air sickness may decide to fly helicopters.

Oddly enough, travel sickness sufferers have a better time of it in helicopters and old jalopies than they do in jets and smooth Rolls-Royces: a good draught provides much-needed oxygen and a rickety ride better matches the human motions of walking and running.

On the road, non-suffering relatives and friends can, with the right tactics, help prevent travel sickness. Adult sufferers like to feel 'in control' and invariably prefer to drive themselves, if possible. Otherwise, they should be offered a choice of seating: some sufferers prefer the back, others the front. Others like to lie down and the desire to sleep, or drowsiness, might persist for a few hours after the journey.

Car windows should be kept open and frequent breaks taken, perhaps for short walks or light meals. Boiled sweets can be effective. A quick dose of glucose restores blood sugar levels lowered by travel tension. Caution is advised about reading, writing or drawing in a car; all these activities can induce nausea. And bright conversation can be a disaster: most sufferers are far too busy repressing the urge to vomit.

Pat: Thanks Maggie, and that's the last time I chat to *you* when I give you a lift home! But really, though . . .

Now listen to the piece again.

TEST ONE: Fourth Part

You will hear a radio report about changes in the English language. For question 12 tick whether you think the statements are true or false. You will hear the piece twice.

Ours is a language which doesn't have an academy telling us what we should or should not say – we like to think that English is the product of more democratic forces, that it belongs to the people who actually speak it. But this hasn't stopped a self-appointed panel of 175 well-known writers, journalists, scholars and public figures meeting recently in the United States to discuss the state of the language.

They last met back in 1969, and their views – expressed in the form of a poll – are taken seriously by lexicographers working for prestigious American dictionaries. The 'experts' include broadcasters William F. Buckley and Alastair Cooke; authors Jessica Mitford, Paul Theroux, Fay Weldon, Isaac Asimov and Carl Sagan; academics John Kenneth Galbraith and Susan Sontag; as well as politicians Jeanne Kirkpatrick and Eugene McCarthy.

What these guardians of the language have to say, though, will not please the purists. The panel members seem to have admitted defeat in the struggle against usage that some consider to be incorrect: rules the 175 used to insist on have been abandoned as trivial and no longer worth fighting for.

This won't please British sticklers either: language fashions are quick to cross the Atlantic and this latest shift has already been branded as 'disastrous' in some quarters; others are more resigned and regard it as a reflection of what they see as 'the decline in cultural literacy'.

Some examples should illustrate the change. In 1969 three quarters of the panel insisted that the verb 'to decimate' could only mean – as in the Roman Legions – to kill one in ten. Now, two thirds accept its current usage as meaning 'to slaughter the majority of'.

Seventy per cent now approve of 'aggravate' to mean 'irritate' – just over forty per cent did so in sixty-nine; while half accept 'anxious' as having the same meaning as 'eager' – compared with less than a quarter in the sixties.

The use of 'transpire' to mean 'happen' is regarded as acceptable by 58 per cent, and in fact half of the experts said that its original meaning – 'to become known' – should now be dropped altogether.

Grammatical correctness is now being seen as a rather conservative attitude, and although the panelists did hold out against the mixing of singular and plural forms in sentences such as 'everyone who works here has their own office', we can expect furious reactions from the protectors of linguistic purity when they realise that half of the experts refused to condemn the split infinitive: 'to quickly run', or, in the immortal words of Star Trek – 'to boldly go'.

Now listen to the piece again.

TEST TWO: First Part

You will hear some information for passengers before an aeroplane takes off. For question 1 you should fill in the missing details. You will hear the piece twice.

Chief Steward: Welcome aboard our Boeing 737. We would ask you, for your comfort and safety, to comply with safety regulations: to place any hand luggage under the seat in front of you, or in the overhead lockers. Your hand luggage must not obstruct the aisles or emergency exits.

We'll be coming through the cabin with landing cards: you do not require these cards if you're in direct transfer to an international flight or if you've a European Community passport.

Pilot: Thank you ladies and gentlemen, I'm Greg Foster the captain; welcome aboard. I'm sorry about this delay, which has been caused by daytime air traffic control restrictions, and then a small technical snag that we had on the aeroplane at Heathrow, but we're ready to go now, just waiting for air traffic control to let us taxi away.

Flying time 45 minutes and we shall be flying at a cruising height of 28,000 feet. Flying conditions are superb, as are the landing conditions in London. So can I invite you to sit back, relax and enjoy your flight.

I will of course speak to you later on during the flight, but meanwhile if there's anything I can do for you please let me know.

First Officer: Cabin crew: doors to automatic please.

Chief Steward: Chief Steward Williams, ladies and gentlemen. This announcement contains important safety information.

In your seat you have a safety card, which contains details of escape routes, oxygen masks and life jackets. Please study it carefully.

The emergency exits are on both sides of the aircraft. There are two doors at the rear and two doors at the front. In the unlikely event of having to use an escape slide, please leave all hand luggage behind and ladies remove high-heeled shoes.

Please now make sure your table is folded away, your seat back is upright and the arm rest down, and your seat belt fastened.

Thank you for your attention. We wish you a happy flight.

Now listen to the piece again.

TEST TWO: Second Part

You will hear an extract from a radio programme in which three people discuss whether rock music should be taught in schools. For each of the questions 2–6, tick one of the boxes A, B, C or D. You will hear the piece twice.

Bill: . . . . . . well, let's look, shall we, at the examples which were given to us; though I don't think the choice of Guns 'n' Roses is entirely fair but it's the only rock one we've been played so er . . . . .

Steve: It's played all the time on MTV too . . .

Bill: so er . . . what I'm saying – and I'm sure Paul, who's a professional guitarist, will back me here – is that you don't have to be Bach to go from a G to a D seventh 'cos even though Guns 'n' Roses are hardly the most, er the most sophisticated band in the world, I think it's quite possible they've shifted from a G to a D seventh . . . .

Paul: I think it's . . . .

Bill: . . . . once or twice.

Paul: I think it's quite possible they've never done anything else, to be honest.

Bill: Thanks a lot Paul . . . But well if it's sophistication that counts, well then in jazz there's . . . .

Pres: Let's leave jazz for now, Bill . . .

Bill: . . . . so many examples of . . .

Pres: Bill I'm sorry but I must interrupt you there. Can we just make, er can we say a last few words on whether you think children should learn about rock and pop music in schools. Right Paul, you first:

Paul: I can't see any harm at all in studying pieces like 'Yesterday' or er that Bryan Adams one 'Everything I do' – to take a rather more recent example – instead of something from nineteenth-century operetta.

Pres: Steve, what's wrong with putting good popular music on the curriculum?

Steve: The risk is that the little time that is spent on music in schools would be taken up more and more by pop and although some of it is certainly of quite a high standard, children do get lots of exposure to it outside the education system. Unfortunately, this is not often the case with classical music, and many young people would grow up without ever learning about the vast range of music that we have inherited from earlier centuries, and indeed which modern styles of music have developed from.

Pres: Bill?

Bill: I'd like to see children being shown – through well-chosen examples – that every kind of music has something to offer, well that in their different ways they all have a contribution to make to learning.

Pres: Right, well we really must leave it there but I can see that you want to carry on discussing outside the studio: so, thanks the 3 of you.

Now listen to the piece again.

TEST TWO: Third Part

You will hear an extract from a radio programme in which ways of avoiding global warming are suggested. For question 7 tick whether you think the statements are true or false. You will hear the piece twice.

Presenter: So what can we actually do about this heating up? Fred Pearce has been looking at some pretty strange solutions to climatic catastrophe offered by scientists.

Fred: If the world gets too hot, we should put up a parasol. The logic is impeccable; the design of the parasol comes from a Swiss boffin called Walter Seifritz. Last autumn, Seifritz proposed that we should hoist into space a giant aluminium shade 20 times the size of Britain. The 45 million-tonne parasol would hang in space at a point where it would blot out enough sun to cool the world by 2.5 degrees centigrade.

The cost, in easy payments over 20 years, would about equal current global military spending.

Since the greenhouse effect hit the front pages, all manner of boffins have offered their pet solutions. Dr Wally Broecker of Columbia University, New York, suggested mimicking large volcanic eruptions, which pour dust and gases such as sulphur dioxide into the upper atmosphere, to cool the planet by shading the surface. A fleet of 700 jumbo jets spraying the stratosphere around the clock would do it. The bill: $10 billion a year.

Painting the world's deserts white would make them reflect more of the sun's heat into space. Filling the oceans with white polystyrene balls would have the same effect.

More sophisticated is the notion of recycling the carbon dioxide that we pour into the air from power stations and car exhausts. There are grand schemes for removing the gas as it goes up power station chimneys, liquefying it and pouring it into salt mines or the ocean.

Or we could grow more algae, which absorbs a third of the world's carbon dioxide. This would mean adding some sort of fertiliser to the oceans. American researchers say an extra ration of iron filings poured on to the water would also help, since in some parts of the Pacific Ocean algae run short of iron.

Ivan Jaques from the University of Chile suggests algae farms: giant lagoons along coasts. 22 million hectares of them, less than half the area of the North Sea, would soak up the carbon dioxide surplus.

But what would we do with all the algae? One solution would be to recycle it, by converting it into fuel for car engines and power stations. The same might be done with trees, which absorb large amounts of carbon dioxide as they grow. Again, scientists have had their calculators working overtime. One American power company recently volunteered to pay for 52 million trees to be planted in Central America – enough to soak up all the carbon dioxide produced by its latest power station during its 40 years of operation.

Presenter: Well, plenty of imagination there, but what about . . .

Now listen to the piece again.

TEST TWO: Fourth Part

*You will hear some advice on how to make money by writing books. For each of the questions **8–12**, tick one of the boxes A, B, C or D. You will hear the piece twice.*

Presenter: . . . and talking of New Year, how about one big resolution? Over to John.

John: Why not make it the year you write a book? No, it's all right – you don't have to worry about plot structures and characterisation: we're talking easy money here. The book you write will be used by others, less resolute than yourself, who still think there's an evens chance they can give up smoking, get fit, lose weight or get the top job.

They're wrong of course, but the title of your book – The Total Slob's Way to Total Fitness; Think Millions, Make Millions will be enough to convince them that this time they can crack it.

Now I know what you're sayng: 'But what if nobody wants to publish my book?' This is what we in the positive thinking business call *negative thinking*. You forget that this is the year that those few publishers without a self-help imprint realise that the biggest market . . . is in self-help.

But before you sit down to write, it's as well that you understand a few basic rules. Luckily for you I've compiled them into a new self-help book: *The Greedy and Lazy Illiterate's Way to a Publishing Fortune*, some secret tips of which I'm now able to offer here.

Get the title right! The perfect title is one that suggests that in 30 painless seconds a day you can remedy some serious defect in your life which, had not the author been willing to divulge his little-known secret, would take superhuman willpower, major surgery or 10 years in analysis to deal with.

Michael Spira's Penguin, *How to Lose Weight Without Really Dieting*, is an example to us all. I know you need to eat less to lose wight, so do you. So, I imagine, does Dr Spira. It hasn't stopped the book going into a reprint and a second edition.

Don't write too much! There are two reasons for this. First, self-helpists are only interested in thin books. Fat books suggest that their life-cure may not be complete by the time the pubs open. Second, self-help books invariably only have one very short idea. Take Dr Spira's seminal diet-less weight-loss book, for instance. What the book says is summed up in the introduction: 'Eat less . . . but only a little less.' It takes 181 pages to make the point though. Or, rather, and here's another self-help secret, abut 130 pages once you knock off the index, weight charts, recipes for toast and honey and toast and marmalade (a page in themselves) and so on.

Go where the market is! Diet books were the most popular sellers of the Eighties, but at the moment the big sellers are New Age and self-help books. And it seems that the two areas in which people most want help are in curing stress and getting married.

Stress books say two things: lie down for half an hour, or go for a run round the block and then lie down for half an hour. I'm sure you could get a couple of hundred pages out of that. Marriage books currently concentrate on getting a man and keeping him. Books on getting a woman and keeping her are, in the trade, generally considered too tacky for publication.

And a final word: remember that the real big sellers at the moment are self-help recordings, so, if you really can't write, put it on a tape!

Presenter: Thanks John, and now . . .

Now listen to the piece again.

TEST THREE: First Part

*You will hear a radio interview on the subject of punctuality. For questions **1–5** tick one of the boxes A, B, C or D. You will hear the piece twice.*

Presenter: Now here right on cue is Jenny, and today she's going to talk to us about her pet hate, which is: people who never turn up on time.

Jenny: A friend once said to me that people who are continually late are like murderers. The only difference between the two is that a murderer robs you of your entire life in one go, while a latecomer robs you of little bits of your life, every day. And I've got some sympathy with this argument, like for instance when . . .

Presenter: But how did you come to feel so strongly about this? Was there something that made you . . .

Jenny: Well yes, you see, when I was growing up my father prided himself on calculating the time by the sun. This would have been a very useful skill but for the fact that his job as an electrical contractor meant that he spent most of his working day underneath a set of floorboards. This had rather an unfortunate effect on his punctuality and – in the end – on his marriage to my mother . . .

Presenter: Really! But surely you can't put everyone into the neat little categories of punctual and unpunctual? Aren't we all sometimes a bit late . . .

Jenny: No. You see, the world's divided into those who are on time, and those who are not: what I call the Sticklers and the Amblers. The Stickler runs from place to place in a panic, catching sleeves in doors. In doing so she is expressing, first, a great respect for other people's time, and, second, a slight inferiority complex; a feeling that if the deadline isn't met, the world will move on without her.

The Ambler, on the other hand, strolls into appointments 20 minutes late. He arrogantly believes that any schedule can be manipulated to suit himself – so why worry? But the time that his victim spends waiting is dead time. If you begin a meeting, you later waste time recapping. And there is absolutely nothing in this world of any value you can do, even for five minutes, on a freezing street corner when it's sleeting . . .

Presenter: They're starting to sound like . . .

Jenny: No don't get me wrong, they don't *see* themselves as selfish: it's just that they don't have any sense of time allocation – what I mean is they give themselves ridiculous schedules, as in 'I'm just going to mow the lawn, clean the bathroom, pop to the shops and watch that film I've taped. I'll be round in 10 minutes'. And if you question their judgment, they respond with anger and denial. Contrary to current counselling recommendations, the response I then find most useful is a punch in the face.

There'll always be Sticklers and Amblers, just as surely as there is Left and Right – and, just as the weak is drawn to the strong so the Stickler will be drawn towards the Ambler. She will marry him, and she'll grind her teeth to powder for the rest of her days. Believe me: I know what I'm talking about.

Presenter: Spoken with feeling, Jenny – but I can't help thinking of John Cleese in *Clockwise* and what can happen to a Stickler if plans go wrong . . .

Now listen to the piece again.

TEST THREE: Second Part

You will hear one half of a telephone conversation. For questions 6–11 fill in the missing information in the spaces provided. For questions 12 and 13 tick one of the boxes A, B, C, or D. You will hear the piece twice.

5080?
Alright Jeff.
Not so bad; and yourself?
Great – and about time too. Well, what can I do for you?
The video . . . hang on I'll just get a pencil and make a few notes . . . uh-huh . . . it's a Sony isn't it?
Oh right, a Sanyo – which one is it? GD nine-oh-two-eight: got that.
OK, what's up?
Just lines and no sound . . . yeah.
Well I know it sounds daft but have you checked out the lead, you know the one to the back of the telly?
Mmm.
And what about the plug – no loose . . . look sorry to be a pain but you wouldn't believe how often it really is something like that . . . right . . . Telly itself? Fine.
OK – is the mains switch handy?
Right.
Just switch off for a few seconds, will you?
That'll do.
Oh don't worry about the clock for the moment; put it back onto the video channel . . . that should be the highest number . . . right, on sixteen then . . . and try the picture.
No better?
All right then, let's try something else. Can you take the tape out and press "play".
Uh-huh.
What have you got on the screen?
Well it's tuned in OK then.
Look, how long ago did you buy it?
Hmmm
And when was the last time you got the heads cleaned?
Yeah, like a tape deck. You don't mean that in four and a half years you haven't . . .?
Yeah I've got one here you can borrow.
Oh that's alright.
No, no . . . glad if I've helped.
See you, bye.

Now listen to the piece again.

TEST THREE: Third Part

You will hear about a study comparing British women with women in a number of countries. For question 14 tick whether you think the statements are true or false. You will hear the piece twice.

It's been called the New Demographics and it's a way of classifying women according to their way of life. Four groups of women found all over the world have been identified: first the 'stay-at-home housewives' – the oldest and least educated group, those following the traditional roles of wives and mothers. Then there's the 'plan-to-work housewives' – women who are generally younger and better educated and who, while devoted to their children, are looking forward to working. Among those who've actually got jobs are the 'just-a-job working women': those who are financially motivated to work but also find satisfaction in the social interaction of the workplace; and finally there's the 'career women' – the best educated and most affluent group, who find in work a sense of achievement.

Although more women are going to work in all the countries studied, the ratio of working women to housewives in the population varies widely, from 55% in the USA to 27% in Brazil. The British figures are 47% working to 53% staying at home, but these are 1981 figures and there has been a considerable increase in women working since then. Attitudes of housewives towards full-time jobs vary widely. The proportion of 'stay-at-homers' is larger in the UK than in any of the other 10 countries – nearly three out of four opt to stay at home compared with only one out of four in Brazil. In every country except Canada and Venezuela women in paid employment are more likely to see their work as just-a-job than as a career.

Taking career orientation and desire to work among housewives as a measure of women's ambition and aspiration, Brazil is the country with the greatest potential for change while Germany has the least. Although women in Britain do not seem particularly career-oriented or aspirational – 37% are stay-at-home housewives and 30% see work as just a job – this is not because they believe that children should be the focus of their lives. Only 14% of British women say that a woman needs children to be fulfilled, compared with 46% in Italy, though over half believe children are important to a happy marriage. In fact, women in the UK are less likely to have children than women in any other country except Japan.

Now listen to the piece again.

TEST THREE: Fourth Part

You will hear a radio programme about health. For questions 15–19 tick one of the boxes A, B, C or D. You will hear the piece twice.

Presenter: It is painful, it is fashionable and more than one surgeon thinks that its incidence may be exaggerated. But sufferers have no doubts:

Patient 1:   The pain in your hands never goes away.

Patient 2:   It's like somebody trying to pull a muscle out.

Presenter: The most obvious symptom of tenosynovitis is excruciating pain in the hands and arms, which can be long-lasting. The Department of Health recognises tenosynovitis as an industrial disease that can be caused by 'any job involving manual labour or repeated movements of the hand or wrist'. A brief guidance note issued in 1977 describes it as this country's 'second commonest prescribed disease' citing assembly-line work and conveyor-belt food-sorting as examples of processes where it is widespread. Recently there have been instances of it among white-collar workers using electronic keyboards and supermarket checkout staff passing bar codes on goods packets over scanners. These apparently simple facts are now the source of controversy, heightened by the large sums employers could have to pay out to tenosynovitis sufferers. Campbell Semple, a hand surgeon.

Semple: The department definition of tenosynovitis is unfortunately very broad. In the vast majority of these legal cases, the initial seed is sown when the patient has an initial vague ache in the hand or forearm, often before any diagnosable signs are present, and the factory doctor or general practitioner writes 'tenosynovitis' on the sick certificate.

Presenter: Mr Semple thinks this leads to an exaggerated idea of prevalence of tenosynovitis, and can cause patients to believe they have it when they do not. It is a view echoed by John Varian, in whose experience a third of such patients suffer from a form of hysteria or occupational neurosis. These people are neither malingerers nor frauds but are swept up in union-backed compensation claims:

Varian: They *believe* themselves to be suffering from such a condition, they actually feel the pain.

Presenter: These are of course convenient arguments for employers and insurers. Both Mr Semple and Mr Varian appear in court on their behalf. Health and safety campaigner David Gee.

Gee: It's not a new approach. It seems simpler for many doctors to say there must be something wrong with the way they are expected to work.

Presenter: Orthopaedic surgeon Rodney Pell uses the term repetitive strain injury, or RSI, to describe the phenomenon.

Pell: People are having to do the bits and pieces machines can't do. And this is repeated for long hours with long retained posture – often with fine little finger movements as in assembly, or just gripping and pushing stiff material such as cardboard. The result can be irreversible damage due to changes in tissues that are not yet properly defined.

Presenter: However, Mr Pell himself does not discount psychological factors and is all too aware of the harmful effect of protracted medico-legal controversy on the patient who is pursuing a claim for damages.

Now listen to the piece again.

TEST FOUR: First Part

You will hear a number of gift suggestions for travellers. For question 1 tick one of the boxes A, B, C or D next to the correct picture. For questions 2–4 tick one of the boxes A, B, C, or D. You will hear the piece twice.

From all the glittering but ultimately useless presents vying to attract the last-minute shopper, I've plucked the following selection: guaranteed to make the recipient's heart grow fonder when he or she is furthest from your side.

The driving traveller might find a foldaway tool kit invaluable: a pair of pliers for those emergency wiring jobs, an adjustable spanner that'll loosen or tighten just about anything anywhere, and a good solid screwdriver with three different-sized blades. All for £12.40 from Motorfix, 18 Borough Road, SE18.

Small but handy, the mountaineering-hook key ring makes a good stocking filler. Silver grey, it is light to carry but so strong that the weight of an adult can be held by the hook end. Price £14.95, from Presents, 129 Sloane Street, SW1.

For those who like to keep in touch with world affairs, Sony has the ICF 2001 D Portable World Radio. It can be pre-programmed for up to 32 stations, boasts a wealth of extras – including a clock and various alarm calls – and is slim, compact and relatively light at 4 lb. Price £299, from Sony dealers.

Keen travelling fishermen will appreciate the Hardy Smuggler – a 9 foot 5 inch rod that folds down to a four ounce, seven section package. It's made of carbon fibre, comes in a partitioned rod bag and costs £209. An additional leather carrying case costs £52.20. Reel and lines are extra. From the House of Hardy, 61 Pall Mall, SW1, or call 839 5515 for nearest stockists and mail-order.

For high fliers who like to write as well, the Pelikan fountain pen is elegant, slim and reliable under stress; it won't leak in the top pocket under the pressure that aircraft travelling inflicts and is reputed to be the first pen not to do so. Price £220, from Mansfield, 30–35 Drury Lane, WC2 and most leading stationery outlets and pen specialists nationwide.

For the very elegant traveller, a complete jewellery case with all the compartments she could want. Pressed leather with a mock-croc finish, it looks like a briefcase, weighs only about a pound and will pop easily into the hotel safe and keep everything just so. Price £849, from Joseph, 26 Sloane Street, SW1.

A travelling essential is the Boots Expedition Kit, which comes in a plastic zipper bag and contains: antiseptic creams, waterproof dressing strip, a triangular bandage, blister kits, scissors, tweezers, insect repellent – 15 different things in all. Price £9.99, from branches of Boots.

A really comfortable mobile bed has to be a great gift for travellers. Hermès version, however, is only for the well-heeled. It's made from pear wood, lateral supports in natural or black cowhide and the angle of tilt at both ends is adjustable. It weighs a little over 44 lb and the price is about £5,000, from Hermès, 55 New Bond Street, W1.

Now listen to the piece again.

TEST FOUR: Second Part

You will hear a telephone recording which gives advice to consumers on how to deal with sales techniques. For questions 5–9 tick one of the boxes A, B, C or D. You will hear the piece twice.

Welcome to the *Sunday Times Guideline*. I'm Cassandra Kemp, consumer affairs editor of *Good Housekeeping* magazine, here to tell you what you should know about door-to-door sales.

Many reputable firms sell their products on a door-to-door basis, but there are still a few unscrupulous traders out there who will take advantage of you; and pressurise you into buying something you don't really want, or could have got more cheaply somewhere else. Here are some of the things you should watch out for.

People trying to convince you you're at some kind of risk, perhaps from burglars because of inadequate security, or because they claim the tiles are coming off your roof and need fixing. High-pressure sales talk, where a salesman will wear down your resistance, sometimes over a period of hours, until you take the easy way out and agree to buy. The showhouse technique, where you're offered an alleged discount because your house will be used as a show house for their double-glazing, exterior paint or whatever. The discount-only-available-tonight technique, which is designed to make you sign up, without having the chance to check prices elsewhere. The hard-luck story: 'I'll lose my job if I don't make my quota of sales this month' – bad luck.

If you want to buy from a doorstep salesman, check the following things. That you know what you're getting. That you couldn't get it more cheaply elsewhere. That you know how much you're spending in total: if you're buying on a finance agreement or buying something like a set of books over a period of time, be absolutely sure of the final cost. If you buy in your home, you have the normal rights regarding the product and its performance. If you decide to buy, then change your mind, you may be able to take advantage of a cooling-off period during which you can get any deposit back. Check this too before you sign anything.

Many companies which sell by this method are members of the Direct Selling Association, and comply with their code of practice. They guarantee everything they sell, and give you 14 days to cancel any order if you want to. For a list of their members, or to get further information, contact them at: 44, Russell Square, London WC1B 4JP; that's 44, Russell Square, London WC1B 4JP. Thank you for calling *Guideline*.

Now listen to the piece again.

TEST FOUR: Third Part

You will hear a radio programme about graffiti artists. For question 10 tick whether you think the statements are true or false. You will hear the piece twice.

Presenter: Mark Jackson is a London-based graff-ite: a graffiti artist who learned his trade on the capital's concrete and steel. This month, the Italian publishing house Stanta Alter Nativa took Jackson and four other spraycan stylists on a week-long series of performances in Europe. It was the prelude to a 15-artist, 14-date show which will tour Italy later this summer.

Mark: I've never been in a rock band or anything like that, but I found being on tour was like being a pop star – the lifestyle was pretty much what I'd imagined. Everything's provided, with three- and four-hour shows to fill, and big parties after every one.

Presenter: Jackson, a 28-year-old refugee from advertising art, says the jaunt opened his eyes:

Mark: In Paris, London graff-ites who work there are funded by arts councils. In Amsterdam it's legal, and they work on metal shutters. We got more attention over four days in Milan than we had in London in three years.

Presenter: Officialdom in Europe is more tolerant to graffiti than it is in Britain.

Mark: In Milan you can just reach out and tag a train. We even pieced in broad daylight.

Presenter: To 'piece' or create a work – from 'masterpiece; – and to 'tag', or embellish with one's signature, are lynchpin terms in the verb-heavy vocabulary of London Graff-ites, who know and respect each other's tags. Mark Jackson, also known as Contempt, again.

Mark: Walking around, you'll think of people's names, tags that are up on walls and trains. You get to know people you'll never meet, find out where their manor is. You make friends without ever getting to meet.

Presenter: Those forbidden UK stylings which fascinate Europeans are older than many Britons think. Ricky Plant, whose *nom de graff* is Chase, is the man who taught Jackson how to wield the cans of spray.

Ricky: We're coming up to the third wave of London graff-ites now. Back in 1981 I saw a film called *Wildstyle*, saw some real pieces in that and thought 'I've just got to do it'.

Presenter: So, like other would-be British graff-ites, Plant bought a copy of Martha Cooper and Henry Chalfont's American photobook *Subway Art* and hit the streets to teach himself.
Plant has been prosecuted for his art. In court, the prosecutor held up a photo-enlargement of the offending piece and sternly asked the graff-ite how he felt:

Ricky: 'I think it holds up', I said, 'even in black and white'.

Presenter: Today, Plant, like crewmates Jackson and Sandra 'Syanide' Belgrave, is 'legal'; he executes commissions for business cards. TV shows, shopfront windows, concert decor, even interiors.

Ricky: Abstract graffiti looks really killer on the right wall in the right flat.

Presenter: Graduate graff-ites can be authoritative on questions of style, stressing the 'interconnectedness' of British fashion, sound and sport.

Ricky: Where I live in West London, everything interlocks; you look at some graff and its letters are really angular. Then you look at the designer shoes people wear and their lines are just the same. DJs can draw, skaters make videos, mixers know how to dress.

Presenter: In this world, artists can 'scratch-mix' on a Xerox machine as well as on a record turntable, the dance floor is a visual as well as an audio sphere.

Ricky: Before it grows up, style always comes from the street, but guys on the street never get that recognition.

Presenter: To raise the public's consciousness about who initiates trends, Plant, Jackson and Belgrave last year staged two exhibitions of graff-ite art at West London's Tabernacle Community Centre. Among the most attentive guests were local policemen keen to match tags and faces.

Ricky: They scared a lot of our artists away from the reception on opening night . . .

Now listen to the piece again.

TEST FOUR: Fourth Part

You will hear a women's radio programme about getting revenge on ex-lovers. For question 11, tick the boxes to show which suggestions are made. For question 12 tick one of the boxes A, B, C or D. You will hear the piece twice.

Presenter: Hi everyone; this morning we're looking at ways of getting revenge on that two-timing man who made your life a misery: like the woman who this week kicked up a stink after her lover dumped her – by secretly sewing prawns into his curtain lining! The only way to handle a double dealing rat is not to get mad – but get even. So here are some of your ideas read by Pam and Sue.

Pam: Right, well here goes. The first one's an old favourite: hand back the keys to his lovenest – I'm quoting here – and his car: after supergluing the locks.

Sue: How about this one: sprinkle his-deep pile carpets with mustard and cress seeds. Water lightly then turn up the heating for best effect. Should bring out the green in him.

Pam: This one's for the married man: return in a taxi every item of lingerie he has ever bought you. Then tell the driver he is to be paid cash on delivery.

Sue: Here's an idea for when you're moving out – while he's cleared off for the weekend – ring the Australian speaking clock, then take the phone off the hook. Leave him a note which starts 'Dear Bill'.

Pam: An animal lover's sent this one in: remember the cheated wife who got great satisfaction from lacing her husband's weekly curries with dogfood? It made her pet bounce – but not with health.

Sue: A listener from north of the border asks: he likes eggs? She says give him eggs. One spurned lover she knowns placed six at strategic intervals beneath his carpet, then trod them in lightly to produce a horrible and untraceable smell.

Pam: We're asked here to think about the cast-off lover who hit *her* rich romeo rat where it hurts most — in his wardrobe. She burned *one* of each pair of his handmade Italian designer shoes.

Sue: This one tells the tale of the woman who put a red towel in the hot wash with her bloke's favourite shirts and undies. Left him looking a bit off-colour.

Pam: My last one's this: record over his football videos with a Barbara Cartland mini-series and wipe that smirk off his face.

Sue: So to end with: light a fire – with his address book, diary and football season ticket. All the things that bring back the warmest memories!

Naturally, we wouldn't want *you* to try these, girls . . .

Ok then, if you've got any other good ideas for getting your own back on cheating ex's, just drop us a postcard clearly marked 'Love Rats' at this address . . .

Now listen to the piece again.

ANSWER KEY

TEST ONE

Paper 1—Reading Comprehension

Section A – one mark for each correct answer.

1 D	2 B	3 A	4 B	5 D	6 B	7 C	8 A	9 A	10 C
11 B	12 A	13 D	14 A	15 B	16 A	17 C	18 B	19 D	20 B
21 C	22 D	23 A	24 D	25 C					

Total: 25

Section B – two marks for each correct answer.

26 D	27 B	28 C	29 D	30 A	31 A	32 B	33 A	34 A	35 D
36 C	37 B	38 A	39 B	40 B					

Total: 30

Paper 3—Use of English

Section A

Question 1 – one mark for each correct answer.

1 prescription **2** out **3** label **4** off **5** through **6** neither **7** taken **8** hand **9** must **10** are **11** by **12** This **13** coming **14** from **15** put **16** by **17** likely, inclined **18** on **19** Indeed/Moreover **20** no

Total: 20

Question 2 – one mark for each word or phrase between the vertical lines, or more marks where shown. Ignore the words printed in *italics*.

a *Who did* | the vehicle belong to before/previously? |

b *Do* | that again and | *you'll be in serious trouble.*

c *However* | much you invest in the business, it | much you invest in it, the business | *will never make money.*

d *To prevent* | livestock (from) straying onto the road, | *a fence was put up.*

e *Not to* | have taken | *the extra supplies* | would have made | them fail. |/ would have led | to them failing. | would have stopped etc | them succeeding. | (3 marks)

f *Only after* | relatives had been informed were the victims' names | made public/released. | (2 marks)

g *He asked her what* | she had been up to | the night before/the previous night. | (2 marks)

h *The Chairman wishes* | me to speak | *to you on his behalf.*

Total: 12

Question 3 – one mark for each word or phrase between the vertical lines. Ignore the words printed in *italics*.

a *We needn't go into details. Suffice* | it to say | *that an accident has taken place.*

b *They seized several hostages and are reported* | to be/have | *headed south.*

c *He threatened* | to report them/to go | *to the police unless they turned the music down.*

d *I was shocked by what we saw but she looked as if she* | couldn't care/couldn't have cared | *less.*

e *Were there* | to be | *any further incidents, stronger measures would have to be considered.*

f *What a childish way to carry on! Why can't you* | act your | *age?*

Total: 6

Question 4 – one mark for each word or phrase between the vertical lines. Ignore the words printed in *italics*.

a | He did that in the belief | *(that) he was helping people.*
     It was his belief | *(that) he was helping people when he did that.*

b | He didn't quite succeed | in breaking | *the world record.* (2 marks)

c | There remains | *an awful lot to do./An awful lot* | remains to be done.

d | There is | *just over a week* | to go before/to/until | *polling day.*
     | *Just over a week* | to go | and | *it will be polling day.* (2 marks)

e | She's experienced enough (as) a player | not to fall | *into that trap.*
     | She's got enough experience as a player | (2 marks)

f They (will) face charges of | *fraud and tax evasion.*
g | Prior to his | appointment as Chancellor | *he worked in the Treasury.* (2 marks)
h | Seeing (as/that) there's nobody else here | *let's go home.*
Total: 12

Section B
Question 5 – the mark shown for each question for coherent and relevant answers, not necessarily echoing the wording given here.

a	To have fun in a convertible (1), it was cheap (1).	2
b	Pictures of members and their cars (1), a short text about them (1).	2
c	A private advertisements section for people looking for partners (1).	1
d	Someone really fed up with (1) travelling to and from work (1).	2
e	He bought a badge (1), placed a regular order for a magazine (1), got some MG underwear (1).	3
f	They ate (1) and drank (1).	2
g	It is used ironically (1), it is almost impossible at first (1), you will often need to do it (1).	3
h	Get it rebuilt (1) bloody (1).	2
i	Refused to start (1).	1
j	By letting water the out (1). His girlfriend left him (1).	2
k	They should be looked at (1) and worked on (1).	2
l	He thinks these people are fanatics/to show his contempt (1).	1
m	An example of a car which seriously damages the environment (1).	1
n	If you haven't yet been put off by all this (1).	1

o One mark each for inclusion of the seven following points, plus an impression mark of 0–3 for a well-expressed, cohesive paragraph, penalising irrelevance, indiscriminate lifting and subjective comment:
+breakdown on first trip with club;   +major engine repairs;
+flat battery;   +poor starting in wet weather;
+problems taking battery out;   +wet interior.
+major bodywork repairs;

Total: 35   10

Paper 4—Listening Comprehension

1st part: **1** D   **2** C   **3** C   **4** D
           Total: 4
2nd part: **5 a** Lady Macbeth   **b** fingerprints   **c** washed   **d** claustrophobia   **e** Aids   **f** 2 million
           g about 660,000   **h** trains/the train   **i** a spider   **j** black circles
           Total: 5 ($\frac{1}{2}$ mark each)
3rd part: **6** D   **7** B   **8** A   **9** B   **10** C   **11** C
           Total: 6
4th part: **12 a** F   **b** T   **c** T   **d** F   **e** T   **f** T   **g** F   **h** T   **i** T   **j** F
           Total: 5 ($\frac{1}{2}$ mark each)

TEST TWO

Paper 1—Reading Comprehension

Section A – one mark for each correct answer.
  1 B   **2** A   **3** A   **4** C   **5** A   **6** C   **7** D   **8** D   **9** A   **10** D
 11 C **12** A **13** A **14** D **15** C **16** B **17** D **18** C **19** A **20** D
 21 A **22** B **23** C **24** D **25** A
Total: 25

Section B – two marks for each correct answer.
 26 C   **27** C   **28** A   **29** B   **30** D   **31** C   **32** B   **33** D   **34** C   **35** A
 36 A   **37** A   **38** B   **39** B   **40** A
Total: 30

Paper 3—Use of English

Section A
Question 1 – one mark for each correct answer.
1 yet **2** by **3** coverage/reporting **4** Although/While **5** evidence **6** age/era **7** never
8 However/Nevertheless/Still **9** have **10** among(st)/by **11** under **12** held **13** measures
14 could/should/might **15** One **16** at/during **17** in/about **18** given **19** avoid **20** up
Total: 20

Question 2 – one mark for each word or phrase between the vertical lines, or more marks where shown. Ignore the words printed in *italics*.

a *There is* | no denying (the fact) that | *serious mistakes have been made.*
b *The system must be* | seen | to be changing. | (2 marks)
c *The manager was forced to open the safe* | at gunpoint. |
d *Their threat to kill hostages* | has been universally condemned. |
e *He is* | believed | to have resigned | *because of financial irregularities.* (2 marks)
f *There is* | deep division | between | *the two wings of the Party.* (2 marks)
g *If it* | hadn't been | for their warning (us), | *we'd have made exactly the same mistake.* (2 marks)
h *Much* | as/though we regret the closure, there | *really was no alternative.*
Total: 12

Question 3 – one mark for each word or phrase between the vertical lines. Ignore the words printed in *italics*.

a *While we're out, help* | yourself/yourselves to | *any eats and drinks you fancy.*
b *In such a delicate situation, the least* | said the | *better.*
c *He is very clever* | at | *talking people into doing things.*
d *What a nasty thing to do! You* | should/ought to be ashamed | *of yourself.*
e *Eventually he was found, suffering from frostbite* | after wandering etc./after having wandered etc. | *around for days in the Arctic conditions.*
f *I wouldn't go so* | far as to | *say he's a liar, but he certainly tends to exaggerate a bit.*
Total: 6

Question 4 – one mark for each word or phrase between the vertical lines. Ignore the words printed in *italics*.

a | The police shot dead several people. |
　 | The police shot several people dead. |
　 | Several people were shot dead by the police. |
b | How/What about hiring | *a rowing boat for an hour?*
c | Provided she gets/makes a good start, | *I'm sure she'll win.*
　 | Provided she starts well, |
d | There was | a sharp upturn | in | *the value of the country's exports last month.* (3 marks)
e | Extensive modifications have been made to | *the original plan.*
　 | There have been extensive modifications to | (2 marks)
f | Since they gained promotion | attendances have trebled.
　 | Attendances have trebled | since they gained promotion. |
g | He was wrongly accused | of stealing/having stolen | *the money.* (2 marks)
h *Who else* | had access to/could access | *this information?*
Total: 12

Section B
Question 5 – the mark shown for each question for coherent and relevant answers, not necessarily echoing the wording given here.

a Similar nonsense (1).   **1**
b To make money (1); it is not a lot for a "miracle" (1).   **2**
c Some things are much better conductors of heat than others (1); metal is a better one than meat (1); which is better than air (1).   **3**
d One could walk on the charcoal but the pine wood would burn (1), as it is sticky (1).   **2**
e A dance (1); the previous remark was an exaggeration (1).   **2**
f To show what the fire was capable of (NOT what it did) (1).   **1**
g It doesn't actually exist (1).   **1**
h He fell backwards after he had crossed the coals (1).   **1**
i Firewalking (1).   **1**
j It was the less complicated theory (1).   **1**
k Everyone has been taught (1) to keep away from fire (1).   **2**
l He wanted a drink.   **1**
m That is what he would have to do (1).   **1**
n He had been able to see how they did it (1).   **1**
o One mark each for inclusion of the nine following points, plus an impression mark of 0–3 for well-expressed, cohesive paragraph, penalising irrelevance, indiscriminate lifting and subjective comment:
(skeptics)
—they exist to demystify apparently strange phenomena;
—they were concerned that people's gullibility was being exploited;
—they wanted to show that anyone could fire walk.
(not dangerous)
materials　—relatively low heat capacity of wood/charcoal; wood/charcoal a poor conductor of heat; dry wood (i.e. contains little resin) is used;
technique—a few quick steps; toes raised;   **12**
spreading contact over a wide area of the foot.
Total: 32

Paper 4—Listening Comprehension

1st part: **1 b** European Community/EC ($\frac{1}{2}$)   **c** day ($\frac{1}{2}$)   **d** Heathrow/London ($\frac{1}{2}$)
  e London ($\frac{1}{2}$)   **f** 45 minutes ($\frac{1}{2}$)   **g** 28,000 feet (1)   **h** superb ($\frac{1}{2}$)   **i** safety card ($\frac{1}{2}$)
  j 4 ($\frac{1}{2}$)   **k** high-heeled shoes (1).
  Total: 6
2nd part: **2** C   **3** C   **4** A   **5** B   **6** A
  Total: 5
3rd part: **7 a** F   **b** F   **c** T   **d** T   **e** T   **f** F   **g** T   **h** F
  Total: 4 ($\frac{1}{2}$ mark each)
4th part: **8** B   **9** B   **10** A   **11** B   **12** D
  Total: 5

TEST THREE

Paper 1—Reading Comprehension

Section A – one mark for each correct answer.
  1 B   **2** A   **3** C   **4** C   **5** A   **6** D   **7** B   **8** A   **9** B   **10** A
  11 C   **12** B   **13** C   **14** C   **15** A   **16** A   **17** B   **18** B   **19** A   **20** C
  21 B   **22** A   **23** B   **24** A   **25** B
Total: 25

Section B – two marks for each correct answer.
  26 A   **27** B   **28** D   **29** B   **30** B   **31** D   **32** D   **33** A   **34** C   **35** D
  36 A   **37** A   **38** A   **39** B   **40** B
Total: 30

Paper 3—Use of English

Section A
Question 1 – one mark for each correct answer.
1 should **2** such **3** is **4** of **5** This/That **6** in **7** with **8** as **9** do **10** to **11** side
12 reduction/decrease etc. **13** on **14** wasted/spent **15** that **16** as **17** deciding **18** on
19 would/might/could **20** account/consideration
Total: 20

Question 2 – one mark for each word or phrase between the vertical lines, or more marks where shown.
Ignore the words printed in *italics*.
a *If* | he had been able to provide references he would have been | *offered the job.*
b *She smiled* | at him in a friendly way | *as she left.*
c *His plan shows as little business sense* | as it does | *concern for the environment.*
d *It's just* | as well we set out early | or (else) | *we'd have missed the flight.* (2 marks)
e *He's too much* | (of) a competitor | to (ever) give up. | (2 marks)
f *On* | laying off some of the workers, | *the management were threatened with strike action.*
g *No longer* | will employers | be able to | ignore/flout etc. the law. | (3 marks)
h *None* | of the leaders present would comment | *after the meeting.* (2 marks)
Total: 13

Question 3 – one mark for each word or phrase between the vertical lines. Ignore the words printed in *italics*.
a *They were on the point* | of giving | *up when a sudden breakthrough encouraged them to persevere.*
b *The Prime Minister denied being* | out of | *touch with ordinary people's feelings.*
c *I really don't care whether they win or lose; it's all* | the same to | *me.*
d *Into view* | came | *a scene of unimaginable beauty.*
e *The management reserve* | the right to | *refuse admission.*
f *He reached across the table but* | in so | *doing, spilt the water.*
g *Barely* | had they begun/started/managed | *to repair the damage when a second earthquake struck the town.*
Total: 7

Question 4 – one mark for each word or phrase between the vertical lines. Ignore the *italics*.
a | We will know who | has passed (the exam) in September. | (2 marks)
b | The first thing you must do/are to do when you get there is call us. | (2 marks)
c *The food in that place really didn't appeal* | to me. |
d | The time had come to make a fresh start. |/ The time to make a fresh start had come. |
e | Defence spending/ expenditure/the amount spent on defence | is going to be cut | by more than half. |
  (3 marks)

f | Not much/Little etc. has gone wrong | *so far.*
g The chances are (that) she'll win the case. |
h *When she'd finished playing, she put her toys away* | of her own accord. |
Total: 12

Section B
Question 5 – the mark shown for each question for coherent and relevant answers, not necessarily echoing the wording given here.

a We do not expect it to happen (1).	**1**
b Produce a large number (1) of rather odd people (1).	**2**
c They were publicity-seekers (1), or over-imaginative (1).	**2**
d Eliminate from their enquiries (1) the eccentrics (1).	**2**
e To improve their situation temporarily (1), perhaps by being let out of the police station (1); afterwards it may be too late to convince people that they made it up (1).	**3**
f In the first case they believe they are guilty, but not in the second (1).	**1**
g The police (1); it may or may not be true (1).	**2**
h Suggestible ones (1).	**1**
i Range of techniques available (1).	**1**
j People who said they had not committed crimes (1) although it appeared that they had (1).	**2**
k One who withdraws a true confession (1).	**1**
l By getting them to answer a series of written questions about their own personalities (1).	**1**
m Because of a legal detail (1), not necessarily because they were innocent (1).	**2**
n Someone would be wrongly convicted (1); Gudjonsson & MacKeith's work would be made more difficult (1).	**2**

o One mark each for inclusion of the seven following points, plus an impression mark of 0–4 for well-expressed, cohesive paragraph, penalising irrelevance, indiscriminate lifting and subjective comment:

—publicity-seeking;	—they believe what the police say;
—fantasies;	—or because of police pressure, leading to:
—in their short-term interest to do so;	—guilty feelings.
—they actually believe they did it because:	**11**

Total: 34

Paper 4—Listening Comprehension

1st part: **1** B   **2** A   **3** B   **4** D   **5** C
   Total: 5
2nd part: **6** Sanyo ($\frac{1}{2}$ mark)   **7** GD 9028 ($\frac{1}{2}$ mark)   **8** lead   **9** plug   **10** telly/TV/Television
   (8–10 in any order, $\frac{1}{2}$ mark each)   **11** 16 ($\frac{1}{2}$ mark)   **12** B (1 mark)   **13** A (1 mark)
   Total: 5
3rd part: **14 a** F   **b** F   **c** T   **d** F   **e** T   **f** T   **g** F   **h** T   **i** F   **j** T ($\frac{1}{2}$ mark each)
   Total: 5
4th part: **15** C   **16** B   **17** B   **18** C   **19** B
   Total: 5

TEST FOUR

Paper 1—Reading Comprehension

Section A – one mark for each correct answer.

1 C	**2** B	**3** B	**4** B	**5** A	**6** A	**7** D	**8** C	**9** A	**10** B
11 C	**12** D	**13** C	**14** D	**15** C	**16** A	**17** D	**18** B	**19** B	**20** C
21 D	**22** C	**23** C	**24** A	**25** B					

Total: 25

Section B – two marks for each correct answer.

26 B	**27** A	**28** C	**29** D	**30** A	**31** C	**32** C	**33** B	**34** D	**35** C
36 A	**37** B	**38** D	**39** C	**40** A					

Total: 30

Paper 3—Use of English

Section A
Question 1 – one mark for each correct answer.
1 with/by **2** own **3** look/seem/appear **4** pregnant **5** early/soon **6** out **7** was
8 their/normal/proper etc. **9** making **10** with **11** among/in **12** who/that **13** if **14** risk **15** to

16 as **17** attracting/catching **18** however/though **19** over/under/about **20** have
Total: 20

Question 2 – one mark for each word or phrase between the vertical lines. Ignore the words printed in *italics*.
a *She ended* | her speech by thanking | *the organisers.*
b *He warned that only when* | free elections were held | would there be peace. | (2 marks)
c *She needs to be* | fully supported | by you | *if she is to succeed.* (2 marks)
d *The further* | you go, | the greater/bigger etc. the risk. | (2 marks)
e *None* | of the leaders present | would/wanted to etc. comment | *after the meeting.* (2 marks)
f *I had* | terrible difficulty | (in) understanding the first chapter. | (2 marks)
g *He would seem* | to have been fooled | *all along.*
h *They were found in a container* | which/that had been stolen | and left | *alongside the lorry.* (2 marks)
Total: 14

Question 3 – one mark for each word or phrase between the vertical lines. Ignore the words printed in *italics*.
a *Nowadays I don't have time, but I* | used to go | *fishing every weekend when I was younger.*
b *You're overweight, Mr Hill. I'd recommend* | going on/you went on | *a diet now.*
c *I mistook* | you/him/her for | *someone I knew years ago.*
d *He apologised* | for keeping me/us etc. | *waiting so long.*
e *The jury found him guilty* | of robbing/of stealing from | *the bank and the judge passed sentence.*
f *Having caused two road accidents in a month, he was banned* | from driving | *for six months.*
Total: 6

Question 4 – one mark for each word or phrase between the vertical lines. Ignore the words printed in *italics*.
a *She's* | out of form/not in/on (good/her best) form | not playing at the top of her form | *at the moment*
b | Monday's performance is (fully etc.) booked up. |/ All the seats have been booked for Monday night. |
   | All the seats for Monday night have been booked. |
c *It's really* | (got) nothing to do | with him. | (2 marks)
d *The escaped prisoner* | is still at large. |
e *He's been working since 7 am* | without a break. |
f | Is it compulsory | for both of us | *to be there?* (2 marks)
g *The subsidy is* | being phased out. |
h | Unlike him, they hadn't been | Unlike them, he had been | *to that part of town before.*
Total: 10

Section B
Question 5 – the mark shown for each question for coherent and relevant answers, not necessarily echoing the wording given here.

a	Thinking up (1) amusing new schemes (1).	**2**
b	Silliness. (1)	**1**
c	Because flying, according to the writer, is rarely fun (1)	**1**
d	As the passengers must stay in the airport. (1)	**1**
e	That an airline had the original idea. (1)	**1**
f	Because there is no point in their asking where they are going (1) and they can't see for themselves when they get there (1).	**2**
g	The person responsible for Fun-Flying (1) has not considered everything that might happen (1).	**2**
h	Very limited. (1)	**1**
i	While shopping in airports might be pleasurable (1), it surely cannot be that exciting (1).	**2**
j	Because they cannot enjoy the beauty of them (1), one place is indistinguishable from another as they cannot understand the airport announcements (1) and if they are tempted to go outside they will be stopped (1).	**3**
k	Fun-Flying. (1)	**1**
l	Become popular. (1)	**1**
m	Those who travel frequently by plane. (1)	**1**
n	It is expensive (1), airlines never give passengers any useful information (1) and they very seldom get what they want (1).	**3**

o One mark each for inclusion of the following nine points, plus an impression mark of 0–3 for well-expressed cohesive paragraph, penalising irrelevance, indiscriminate lifting and subjective comment:

    (Fun-Flying) —an invention of British Airways
                —passengers are charged £35 and must be at Heathrow by 10am
                —they take a plane without knowing where it is going
                —they must stay in the airport they arrive at
                —they can go shopping there
    (drawbacks) —smaller airports may have a small range of goods on sale
                —duty-free shopping may be more expensive and less convenient   **12**
                —the better the place they land in, the more they are forced to miss
                —people who often fly will find its worst aspects familiar.

Total: 34

Paper 4—Listening Comprehension

1st part: **1** C   **2** A   **3** D   **4** D   2nd part: **5** B   **6** D   **7** A   **8** B   **9** D
        Total: 4   **Total: 5**

3rd part: **10 a** F   **b** T   **c** T   **d** F   **e** F   **f** F   **g** T   **h** T   **i** F   **j** F
        Total: 5 ($\frac{1}{2}$ mark each)

4th part: **11 a**   **b**   **c d**✓ **e**✓ **f**✓ **g**   **h**   **i**✓ **j**   **12** C
        Total: 6 ($\frac{1}{2}$ mark for each box correctly ticked or left blank, 1 mark for 12)

SAMPLE 1

Question 5 – the mark shown for each question for coherent and relevant answers, not necessarily echoing the wording given here.

a   they are not expensive (1); people enjoy being famous for a moment (1); seem very democratic (1)
b   people who are not ordinary members of the public (1)
c   a radio programme (1); its ex-producer rang Green (1); as a joke (1)
d   not the listeners (1); but maybe their presenters do (1)
e   trying to improve their image (1) by pretending to be objective (1)
f   he should have realised it was not as it appeared (1)
g   good, average or poor (1)
h   be too nervous to speak (1)
i   those that might be useful (1)
j   talking to the telephonist or holding the line (1)
k   personal details of the next caller (1)
l   they were rejected by the deputy producer (1); because the people who asked them seemed too uncritical (1)
m   only one chance in ten/10% chance etc of success (1)
n   presenters should interview the bosses of other radio stations (1); to encourage tougher questioning (1)
o   One mark each for inclusion of the five following points, plus an impression mark of 0–5 for well-expressed, cohesive paragraphs, penalising irrelevance, indiscriminate lifting and subjective comment:

Steps	Factors	
—try to get through	—likely to be good performers on the radio	
—answer questions	—ask interesting questions (10)	**Total: 32**
—wait for BBC to call back		

SAMPLE 2

Question 5 – the mark shown for each question for coherent and relevant answers, not necessarily echoing the wording given here.

a   it gradually deteriorates (1)
b   the reasons for this deterioration/decline etc (1)
c   in short, intensive spells (1)
d   it is at its best/it begins to decline (1)
e   used (1)
f   prove to be false (1) when examined closely (1)
g   meeting partners (1); having children (1); shortage of money (1)
h   during one's working life (1) (mention of university etc=0); it will not have precise (or the required) aims (1)
i   people working in different areas are at their best as different ages (1)
j   periods when work is of a lower standard (1); following the age when the best is produced (1)
k   writes fewer papers (1)
l   that people have many ideas early on in their careers (1); Beard said time was needed for experience to grow (1); while Simonton claims time is necessary for ideas to develop fully (1)
m   change career (1)
n   One mark each for inclusion of the five following points, plus an impression mark of 0–5 for well-expressed, cohesive paragraph, penalising irrelevance, indiscriminate lifting and subjective comment:

—deterioration in physical/mental condition	—less work done	
—involved in other activities	—ideas in one area completely developed (10)	**Total: 30**
—diminishing enthusiasm		